RESURRECTING
THE GOSPEL OF JESUS

FROM THE RUBBLE OF RELIGION

THERON MESSER

Notice

This would be a great 12-week study for a small group or an individual believer; discussion questions are built in to the back of each chapter.
Pastor Jim Walters, Bear Valley Church, Lakewood, CO

The cover design and art are the work of Matt Wallen of Form and Function - Visual Communication. www.formandfunctionvisual.com

Unless otherwise noted, the scripture quotations are taken from the *New King James Version* of the Bible copyright 1983 by Thomas Nelson, Inc. publishers.

Jointly published by **Concept Publishing, Inc** and **Book Surge**
a division of the Amazon group of companies.
http://conceptpublishing.org and http://www.booksurge.com

Endorsements:

Theron Messer comes like a grandfather telling stories of our family's history. He takes us over familiar ground but we're surprised to see new sights and discover new meaning to many of the old "homestead" stories in the gospel. The book is scary at points as he shows us how foggy are our understandings of some of those gospel teachings. But the fog melts away as the author brings to the light of day, the core teachings of Jesus that will help us "resurrect" HIS Gospel.
Pastor Jim Walters,   Bear Valley Church, Lakewood, CO

Your book is excellent and I find it intriguing and fresh
Mary Ann Jeffreys, Golden Literary Agency, Golden, CO

This book is true to its purpose providing challenges to one's existing concepts. It is a journey of "Wonder" for anyone willing to explore the life and teachings of Christ.
An anonymous Christian lay person

Thought-provoking, challenging, encouraging and revealing are just some of the words I would use to describe this book. I have known and worked with Theron for years and this book reflects what he lives. I would heartily recommend this book but watch out! It will make you think -- then wonder how on earth you missed some of the simple truths of the Scriptures. This book is for the serious believer who seeks to live His life and reflect His loving heart to hurting individuals
Dr. Scott E. Hadden,   Scope Ministries International

Theron Messer continues to challenge his audience to consider old things in new ways. He turns the tables and sets his readers inside up and outside down. Maybe that's why I like him so much, because we don't need another serving of chicken soup. No, we need spice that will set our minds on fire. If this doesn't resurrect the sleeping mind within, I don't know what will.
Nick Gerlich. PhD, Professor of Marketing, W. Texas A&M University, Canyon, TX

I recommend this book to those who are tired of both hypocrisy and legalism within the church and are seeking a formulation of the Gospel that highlights grace, freedom and union with Christ. Theron Messer brings a wealth of experience as a teacher and counselor to this task. While not agreeing with every point, I was challenged to think more deeply about our experience of freedom in Christ.
Dr. Kenneth Williams,   Pastor, Rockland Community Church, Golden, CO

Acknowledgements

I have chosen to write in a less formal and scholarly format without the inclusion of a myriad of footnotes. Most of the concepts are my own, but as Solomon said, "There is nothing new under the sun." I am an avid reader and have undoubtedly borrowed many ideas from others. My mind is not capable of remembering all the writers who have had an impact on the way I think.

Many people have been my sounding board over the years this manuscript was taking form and it would be impossible to name all of them, but there are several special people without whom I could not have written this book.

First I want to thank Wenda, my wife of nearly fifty years and the mother of our three wonderful children and grandmother of our six amazing grandchildren. We spent many, many hours discussing the various concepts and doctrinal issues presented, and she has taken time from her busy schedule to edit countless drafts of this book. Without her work you would be struggling to read sketchy notes made during my many times of pondering the questions of spiritual life.

I also want to especially thank our children, Randy & Lynette Pickering, Jeff & Heidi Messer, and Aric & Shelley Wallen for their support, love and encouragement.

Many others have been faithful supporters through Grace Ministries and without their help I could not have completed this book. You know who you are! I am especially thankful for Rick Lunnon and Douglas and Jackie Swartz as major financial supporters and for Pastor Jim Walters of Bear Valley Church of Lakewood, Colorado and Dr Ken Williams pastor of Rockland Community Church of Golden, Colorado who critiqued my book and challenged my thinking.

Thank you to our wonderful friends who have been part of our small group, the Quail Ridge Midrash: Chuck & Jelayne Jorgenson, Eric Jorgenson (via e-mail), R.J. & Jennie Gomez, Todd & Beth McWhirter, Aric & Shelley Wallen, Steve & Liz Thompson, Sarah Thompson, Jill Woosley, David Palik and John Garber; and a special thanks to David and to Liz whose many coffee shop discussions with me helped to refine my thinking. You have all challenged and encouraged me and I love you.

I have also been helped and greatly encouraged by my professional editor, Mary Ann Jeffreys of Golden Literary Agency, who read my work and prompted me to publish it.

Table of Contents

Resurrecting the Gospel of Jesus
Introduction

It was a tiny, white, wood-framed church in a town so small that the gas station, village store, and post office were all in one stone building on the two-lane blacktop road that ran through town. Matherton was a backwater fishing site on the Maple River in mid-Michigan. It was there that I first learned about Jesus.

I was a farm boy whose family attended that small United Brethren Church, and I was drawn to the Jesus of my parents' faith. As a child, I knew very little about the Bible, but I knew the Jesus of the gospel stories I heard. He was a kind Savior, a meek and mild King. I also knew Him by His considerable influence over my immediate family and neighbors and His presence in our church family.

Our congregation might swell to fifty people, including kids, on an occasion like Easter Sunday. Otherwise, only five or six families could be counted on to attend the Sunday services. Perhaps the church was of almost no account by usual Christian standards, but we could sing; Oh how we could sing! Our worship services were rich in songs taken from a tattered hymnal, and worshipful singing wasn't reserved for church services alone. One of the same church hymnals was prominently displayed on our old upright piano in the parlor at home.

My grandmother and older sister often played while the entire family sang about Jesus. We also sang on the way to church, usually the song we had just heard that morning on our home radio. The broadcast was from Renfro Valley, somewhere deep in the South, and one song that saturated all we believed and lived was "Precious Memories." Honestly, I learned more about Jesus from the old hymns in those years than I did from the Bible.

Our simple family faith was centered in the love of Jesus. Of course, because we were concerned to never offend this gracious Savior, we had rules to keep, too. But there was love as well as law! I remember, even as a boy, the clash between love and law in our lives. But, you know, love always won. For example, I remember one year when my father had another severe heart attack

7

just after the hay was cut, sun-dried, and raked into rows ready to be taken to the barn. His condition was so severe that he could not load and move the hay. Nevertheless, we all went to church that Sunday morning knowing that a rain storm was moving in and the hay would be ruined in the field.

Our pastor opened the service with prayer, and we sang a song. Then he did something I will never forget. He said that he was convinced that in the Gospels Jesus was more concerned for people's needs than He was for the Sabbath restrictions, and the Lord had told him to dismiss the Sunday service so the men could gather at our farm and harvest the hay before the rain ruined it. Now, this was a Jesus I could love! Jesus cared more for people than He did for religion.

The Jesus of the Gospels, the Jesus I learned to love in my childhood, is such a different person from the Jesus we often hear about in many churches today. The name of Jesus is used to defend our wars, our self-righteousness, and our "religion," but all of these things cause separation. Jesus' teaching centered in relationships. People flock to churches because they are promised a loving community and concerned pastoral care, yet many soon leave because what was promised isn't provided.

Yes, church members smile, shake hands, and sometimes even give a warm hug, but unfortunately, if the "others" who enter the church do not obey the rules and conform to expectations, they often risk being criticized, gossiped about, and treated as outsiders. Churches tend to have revolving doors whereby nearly 50 percent of those who enter are destined to leave in frustration. How can this be the kind of community of love Jesus said would draw all men to Him?

I do not want this to be just another angry attack on the churches of today! I want to see the church survive and thrive. I am only quoting recent research from independent sources and addressing a very real problem. Honesty and change is called for; anger is not.

Many books have been written about the Jesus we do not know today, and I ask myself why I believe I should attempt to write yet another book. The answer in my spirit is that while most of these books feature certain issues about Jesus that have been forgotten by most of Christendom today, they do not go far enough. Why is that? I believe it is because we are afraid to disturb our traditional concepts about Christianity. Tradition has such a hold on us. Many good authors do not tell it all for fear they will be rejected by Christianity's traditional power holders. The dissenters, however, are becoming a majority.

With 50 percent of committed Christians no longer in regular attendance in a church, (see Barna research) we must recognize that the "wineskins" are leaking and the church can't continue to blame the "spilt wine." The problem is with the church and the practice of our traditional Christian religion, and most of us aren't even aware of it. To attack these sacred structures, however, is akin to attacking God Himself. Therefore, we shrink back from the obvious and painful truth in order to preserve the old wineskins.

If you are not familiar with the wineskin analogy, it came from Jesus. In His day He stood firmly against the structure of organized religion. This is what brought about His death. He dared to speak the truth at the expense of the "sacred" structure. Hear His words in Matthew 9:17: "Nor do people put new wine into old wineskins, or else the wineskins break and the wine is spilt, and the wineskins are ruined. But they put new wine into new wineskins and both are preserved."

I long for the existing church to hear the cry of the "spilt wine" (the many believers who are leaving the church). "Patches" (lively, entertaining worship; programs and more programs, etc.) have been placed on "old wineskins" (the church), hoping they will not be cast aside, but the "old wineskins" are still inflexible. Frankly, it is too late for most of the old organizational religious structures. Something new must be birthed by the Spirit to hold the "spilt wine." We need new wineskins, just as Jesus said. Sadly, today's organized church that is run much like a corporation is not all that different from the Pharisaical Jewish religious structure of Jesus' time. The renewed church must be more like an organism than an organization—alive and growing, saturated in grace. It should feature the kind of love I experienced in my childhood church. Something radical must happen for the church to again become the

9

living church of Jesus. Thank God there are some churches and leaders who are becoming aware of this and have begun to prayerfully dialogue about possible change, and in some churches that change is already occurring.

It is not my intent to define the faults of the church or the changes that need to be made, nor do I wish to write another "how to do church" book. Others are doing this. *I want to focus more on how Jesus lived, what He did, and how He related to people; and I want to follow His example.* This refocus on Jesus should automatically correct what we do and how we live.

The Jesus of the Gospels has been buried under so much religiosity that He is not easily recognized today. There is, however, a movement to recommit to the lifestyle of Jesus starting among our youth. In the last decade they were encouraged to wear WWJD bracelets as a reminder to do what Jesus would do. Their question is, indeed, a good one. What would Jesus do? But there is a better question that is dramatically less subjective. What *did* Jesus do?

We are telling our youth that if they will do certain things, they will be spiritual: Have a quiet time, spend a half hour in prayer, attend church, join a small group. All of these may be helpful and powerful disciplines, but they too often reflect form versus substance. They lack the power of a loving relationship at their source. Jesus was a man who related to other people, not a promoter of rules and religions.

We hear sermons on the Jesus who rose early to pray to His Father, but we seldom hear sermons about the Jesus who attended parties and even provided the wine. We hear sermons about the Jesus who never sinned, but we hear few sermons about the Jesus who was very comfortable being with sinners.

Perhaps it is ultimately pure projection to theorize about what Jesus would do today in our culture. It is, however, not theory at all to study what Jesus *did* nearly two thousand years ago. There is a wealth of data in the Gospels to instruct us. It is to the Jesus of the Gospels that we must turn to know *what He would do, based on what He actually did.* I pray that His lifestyle will become fresh and relevant as we review His life and legacy. Over the next 12 chapters I want to introduce you to a very different Jesus from the one that most likely lives in the memory bank of your Christian traditions-programmed brain.

I firmly believe we have been following a Jesus of our own understanding, one generated from Christian traditions, not the Jesus portrayed in the Gospels. In order to correct this distorted view of Jesus, I suggest that we need nothing short of a revised and restored kind of faith, a third-millennium faith. Do not be troubled over my suggestion, because this is not a fantasy Jesus or a Jesus of the past's liberal theology. For this new kind of faith to be distinctly biblical, we need to again be "looking unto Jesus, the author and finisher of our faith" (Hebrews 12:2).

You may be following a shadow savior, a caricature of Jesus, and not even know it. If *your* version of Jesus depicts Him as one who dislikes certain kinds of sinners (especially homosexuals, Muslims, liberals, the divorced, or the addicted), then your faith is twisted by a contemporary caricature of Jesus. How can so many of today's American Christians hate their enemies and assume it is justified, when Jesus told us to love our enemies? Those who hate and look down on others must have the wrong concept of Jesus— the Jesus our traditions have distorted!

In the chapters that follow we will take a closer look at how Jesus lived, and we'll contrast this with today's Christian lifestyle. I will attempt to present many challenging images of Jesus from the Gospels and show that the traditions-laden caricature of Jesus presented by our modern-era Christian church is not the Jesus of the Gospels at all. I will further attempt to show that much of what passes for Christianity is far from Christian, if what we mean by Christian is one who is Christlike.

"Pharisees" still flourish and rule over much of the Christian religion. Modern Christianity is known more for its pharisaical attitude than for the love of Christ. Heaven help us! Be fair minded enough to see that I do not devalue one particular thing about Jesus by placing emphasis on another, perhaps more important, thing. My emphasis is to refocus, not to destroy, valid faith. Be prepared for this and many more challenges.

11

I guarantee you will not read this book and remain unchanged. I do not say this because of what I teach or think—that is not the issue. I simply want to lift up the loving life of Jesus and refocus our faith on—What *Did* Jesus Do? (WDJD). Maybe we will encourage a new bracelet craze. Better yet, maybe we will become a group of people who no longer need an external reminder (like the bracelet), because we will have a vital, internal, spiritual power conforming us to the image of Christ.

Looking to and focusing on Jesus is the most powerful way to really change our lives. It is for this reason that I hope you will prayerfully study every chapter of this book and discuss it with others.

You will probably encounter much personal difficulty as you challenge your own traditional caricature of Jesus. You will most certainly encounter much opposition from well-meaning believers who will warn against your attempts to refocus your own faith. Prayerfully and cautiously persist!

Jesus said, "You shall know the truth and the truth shall make you free." (John 8:32) If what you believe is not the truth, then what you feel is not reality. You will probably have deep emotional reactions when you see your traditions and life in contrast to the life of Jesus. Expect it! If knowing the truth sets us free, then by definition we must be free to follow the truth wherever it leads us.

My premise is that we have a warped reality about our faith because we have a warped view of the person of Jesus. Many others have written on this subject, including Philip Yancey with his great book *The Jesus I Never Knew*, (Zondervan, 1995) So you may rightly ask, why read this book? I suggest that every written picture of the historic Jesus is just one part of a larger puzzle. I believe that my insights are far from exhaustive on this topic but are necessary as a part of what I might call the "rediscovery" of the real Jesus. I also believe that we should take every opportunity to get to know Him better. In this light, let me give you an illustration in chapter 1.

Chapter 1
Lamb Chop or Living Lamb?
Jesus in living reality

I love good food! Especially lamb chops, the best cut of lamb. Just thinking about the finest presentation of this meal makes me salivate! I can easily picture the lamb-chop entree on the classy menu of my favorite restaurant. I know that my taste buds will do handstands over the following:

Spring Lamb Chops carefully rubbed with fresh garden herbs and grilled to perfection. These prime cuts of lamb are served with mint sauce; boiled, early red potatoes; and pearl onions in creamery butter; accompanied by a salad of mixed garden greens laced with our famous raspberry and pecan dressing.

This presentation of lamb may be very attractive and delicious, but it falls dramatically short of knowing a living lamb. A lamb is a warm, wonderful, living creature covered in snow-white cuddly wool, accented with a black nose and feet. Lambs love to run and play. They will quickly bond with you and follow you wherever you go. Domesticated while babies, they willingly become family pets. In the wild they become exciting creatures that run confidently over rocky crags at dizzying heights. They can entertain you for hours with their rock-climbing antics. As the males mature, they become strong, horned rams capable of flattening a person with one running blow delivered with their hard heads.

The lamb chop is just a selectively prepared part of a real lamb. I maintain that this is what most churches present to us today when they give us a palatable but dead version of the Lamb of God. He has been butchered, broiled, and buttered so we'll think that by tasting the "lamb chop" we know the Living Lamb.

The Doctrinal Jesus and the Real Living Lamb

The doctrinal presentation of Jesus is often as dry as eating the menu! The modern-church version of the Lamb of God is presented in such a way as to disguise the death of the creature from which the lamb chops were taken. In a restaurant this is expected. I doubt that any gourmet restaurant will ever present the lamb chops with pictures of the bouncing lively lamb followed by the butcher cutting its throat and shedding red blood over the snowy white wool. This would hardly be appetizing.

In a similar way we have made the person of Jesus into a carefully presented prime lamb-chop plate, complete with parsley, served on expensive china. He is no longer living and exciting, wild and wooly. We enjoy our Sunday gourmet feast and go away full but flat. We do not take home the Living Lamb, let alone discover Him on the rocky crags of the highest mountain peaks called Life.

When you meet the real Living Lamb as He is presented in the Gospels, you will know the vital difference. The doctrinal Jesus and the dissected Jesus are only hints of the real thing. This means that the Jesus of the Gospels still asks us today, "Who do you say that I am?" To rediscover the real Jesus, we must read the limited but powerful presentation of Him in the Gospels with the understanding that Jesus is not an idea but a living person. We say we desire a personal relationship with Him, but one cannot develop much of a relationship with a lamb chop. We need to encounter the whole Living Lamb.

Encountering This Most Unusual Living Lamb

In the Gospels we discover a man who is a provincial Jew, dedicated to His nation and His own people, but we also find that He cannot be contained by Judaism because He is a universal man. His life and death are always presented as being given for the whole world. While it is true that we must discover Him through His Jewish roots, we cannot contain Him in the Jewish family tree. He was simultaneously a traditional Jewish man who used the Old Testament texts with authority and was in absolute submission to the truth contained in them, and also an arrogant agitator against Jewish religious tradition. He was the paradoxical, dedicated defender of the faith of Israel and, at the same time, the indignant

14

insurrectionist against it. He died for the faith while also dying to change it.

Jesus was not a socially acceptable, genial "Mr. Rogers" who was known for always being kind and creating the nice neighborhood. Hardly! He was the meek and mild Lamb who, paradoxically, was also the battering ram who knocked down His people's cultural taboos and offended the accepted social conventions of His day. You will find that Jesus was way too wild a ram to be tamed.

The Untamed Jesus—Wild and Sometimes Offensive

To the chagrin of serious Bible students, we find that Jesus was often soft on sin and hard on self-righteousness. He spoke out in defense of the Law and sanctity of marriage and then protected the adulteress and became friends with the woman at the well who was sleeping around. He instructed Peter and the others to take swords to the Garden of Gethsemane where He was tested before His crucifixion, and then He chastised Peter for using the sword. He taught the value of freedom and then refused to challenge the Roman occupation. For a time He deserted His widowed mother while still claiming that the commandment to honor father and mother was an imperative (see Matthew 10:37 and 12:46-50).

He accumulated a rowdy band of misfit followers who more closely resembled the "Rat Pack" of His day than the kind of people you or I would choose for our pastors. He taught "peace I give to you" and then taught "I have come to bring a sword." He Himself would go without bread for forty days in the wilderness but would make fish sandwiches for thousands so they would not suffer with empty stomachs for just one day. He apparently encouraged Peter to leave his wife to follow Him (Peter had a wife—Matthew 8:14 and 19:27-29) while saying that God expected men to honor their marriage vows for a lifetime. He quickly healed many hurting people and then appeared to callously let His best friend, Lazarus, die. He cried over Jerusalem and cursed Capernaum.

When confronted, He slipped by His enemies and escaped, and He still slips by us today when we try to contain Him, define Him, and present Him like a lamb chop. You may try hard to control Him, but a Living Lamb will not be put on a silver platter surrounded by red crabapples and sprigs of green parsley.

If you wish to pursue the Living Lamb, you will have to leave the doctrinal menu behind and be ready to not only run freely through meadows but laboriously climb risky, rocky mountain trails to follow Him. Your experience will more resemble an unpredictable, exciting journey of fresh discovery than a planned trip that follows a road map. Are you ready?

Jesus Invites Us to Take a Never-Ending, Exciting, and Mysterious Spiritual Journey

At this point you may be asking, what does the lamb chop and Living Lamb analogy have to do with our ability to live like Jesus? Everything! Let me explain it this way. We all enjoy the meadow romp with Jesus, the fluff of Christianity. In essence, Christian Sunday worship services are lamb-chop offerings. We love to sing His praises and worship Him in the church service. This is wonderful (meadow romp stuff), but it will not get you up that dangerous rocky mountain trail. It is dramatically easier to enjoy Him in our safe congregational worship services than to live like Him in our homes, workplaces, dangerous streets, and inner-city ghettos.

Power—The Living Lamb in Us

It takes the Living Lamb fully expressed in us to empower us to live like Jesus. Our objective should be to feast on the Living Lamb so that Jesus Himself might live in us. Paul said it this way: "For me to live is Christ" (Philippians 1:21). If you have been a Christian for some time, you probably know that trying to consistently live like Jesus is impossible. It is not, however, impossible for Jesus to live out His life through us. Let's start the journey of discovery.

The Sacrificial Lamb

The lives of lambs and men have been intertwined since the dawn of creation. No other creature from the animal kingdom has this status in Scripture. In fact, the spiritual mystery of lambs and men appears to predate the creation of our universe (more on that shortly), and we find that the mystery of the lamb will also remain after this earth has been destroyed and the new heaven and new earth have come. The lamb, then, is not as simple as it appears in nature and in the Old Testament. The animal sacrificed for mankind provided the shed blood for forgiveness of sins, meat to eat, and skins to be made into clothing to cover man's nakedness.

The Lamb of God is found in the Bible from Genesis to Revelation. The lamb to which John referred when he called Jesus "the Lamb of God" was the male lamb, the young sheep. It was the primary animal of sacrifice among the Jews. The lamb represented innocence, gentleness, and powerlessness. However, we shall see in the Revelation of Jesus Christ that this gentle Lamb of God was slain and then became the powerful Lamb worthy to rule over all creation. He is found worthy of worship as King of kings and Lord of lords of the whole universe. "Worthy is the Lamb who was slain to receive power and riches and wisdom and strength and honor and glory and blessing" (Revelation 5:12). So what is the process by which this transformation from gentle Lamb to powerful Lamb worthy of worship occurs?

From Helpless Lamb to Ruling Ram
In the spiritual realm of the kingdom of heaven, a major qualification for ruling is that the ruler must first be meek, innocent, gentle, and powerless. Jesus modeled this, as we see in the picture of His triumphal entry into Jerusalem, "Tell the daughters of Zion, 'Behold your King is coming to you, lowly [this is the Greek word also translated meek], and sitting on a donkey, a colt, the foal of a donkey'" (Matthew 21:5).

This characteristic is also to be found in saints who will reign with Christ. It is promised in Matthew 5:5 by Jesus: "Blessed are the meek for they shall inherit the earth." This truly is paradoxical—how can the meek rule? Notice it says, "they *shall* inherit the earth," not they *have* inherited it. We have a revelation of this ruling of the saints in Revelation 5:10 where the slain Lamb makes us, "kings and priests to God; and we shall reign on the

17

earth." This means that the meek saints must somehow mature just as their leader, Jesus the Lamb, did.

We are told in Hebrews 5:8-9 that Jesus Himself had to be made perfect. He was already sinless, so this word does not speak of sinless perfection. Rather, perfect means complete or mature. And how did our Savior become mature? "Though He was a Son, yet He learned obedience by the things which He suffered. And having been perfected [matured], He became the author of eternal salvation to all who obey Him" (Hebrews 5:8-9). If we are meek, we will not be self-seeking, flaunting our power. Jesus became obedient and the servant of all when He, in meekness, surrendered Himself to God and for all mankind. Therefore, we find that self-surrender is necessary for the meek one to rule.

The Lamb Slain from Eternity

The very heart of the throne of God is shown to us by this eternal vision of the slain Lamb who suffered, died, and then was crowned with glory and honor. To be a part of this paradoxical kingdom of heaven, we must be willing to surrender our rights and become meek, just like the little lamb. God Himself has shown us that self-surrender is a universal principle woven into the very fabric of the eternal kingdom. But self-surrender is not demanded of the creatures of the kingdom alone. The Creator Himself submits to the eternal principle by giving Himself for His creation. God in Christ was the slain Lamb by eternal design.

As we, His followers, enter into the act of self-surrender, we surrender our self-directed lives for the absolute control of the One who is creative love personified. By surrendering our lives to Him, we are miraculously translated out of our physical world into His spiritual world, where we participate in the life of the Eternal Lamb, the destiny of the Lamb, the purpose of the Lamb, and the power of the slain Lamb by which He and we overcome death itself.

Eternal Lamb Tracks

We can trace the Lamb from eternity before time to eternity after time, also finding His footprints on the dusty roads of human history. The Lamb willingly giving itself to be slain is an eternal picture of the very character and heart of God. The white wool is a picture of righteousness; the red blood depicts new life and cleansing; and the slain and broken body pictures self-surrender. All are on page after page of the ancient Bible text. Are you beginning to see that there is much more to the lamb than we can contain in a serving of lamb chops? Do you see that "eating one helping" of Lamb (simply asking Jesus to be your Savior and worshiping Him on Sunday) is like only tasting but not feasting on Him?

Where does the pedigree of the Lamb begin? His genetic roots actually extend back before the beginning of time. We catch a glimpse of Him in a key verse, Revelation 13:8, where John introduces the beast who makes war on the saints of God. Some people will worship this beast because he is powerful and awesome. Others do not worship it because they have given their allegiance to another, to the gentle Lamb who controls all things. By this dedication they show that they are the ones whose names have been written in the Book of Life of the Lamb. "The Lamb slain from the foundation of the world" (Revelation 13:8).

Think of this! The Lamb was slain before there was a universe, an ocean, a mountain, or a single human. This Lamb was the source of eternal, timeless life. Jesus, the Lamb of God, offered Himself as the only real meat and the "meal that matters." The life of the Lamb eaten is the meat we eat so we never need kill and eat again. This is the feast of forever! John the apostle did not simply give us this eternal vision, he also gave us the notes from Jesus' essential sermon as He taught in the synagogue in Capernaum. We must take notice of this teaching because it is the central piece interfacing the life of the Lamb with the life of man. This is vintage Jesus in the Gospels.

Eating the Flesh of the Lamb of God

"Most assuredly I say to you, he who believes in Me has everlasting life. I am the bread of life. Your fathers ate the manna in the wilderness and are dead. This is the bread that comes down from heaven, that one may eat of it and not die. I am the living

19

bread which came down from heaven. If anyone eats of this bread, he will live forever; and the bread that I give is My flesh, which I shall give for the life of the world." The Jews therefore quarreled among themselves, saying, "How can this Man give us His flesh to eat?" Then Jesus said to them, "Most assuredly, I say to you, unless you eat the flesh of the Son of Man and drink His blood, you have no life in you. Whoever eats My flesh and drinks My blood has eternal life, and I will raise him up in the last day. For My flesh is food indeed and My blood is drink indeed. He who eats My flesh and drinks My blood abides in Me, and I in him. As the living Father sent Me, and I live because of the Father, so he who feeds on Me will live because of Me. This is the bread which came down from heaven—not as your fathers ate the manna, and are dead. He who eats this bread will live forever." (John 6:47-58)

Jesus Teaches Cannibalism?

Unfortunately for us today, we do not fully appreciate the sickening aversion that Jewish people had to the teaching of Jesus in this text. Many of His followers were so turned off that in John 6:60 we find that they said, "This is a hard saying." In verse 66 we are told that they walked with Him no more. Those who had followed Him to receive their share of miraculous bread (the multiplication of the loaves and fishes) were not willing to exchange common bread for His uncommon flesh. Neither would you or I.

Think about it! Jesus appeared to have just taught cannibalism, a heathen practice that Jews especially abhorred. Jesus responded as the crowd began to move away, "The words that I speak to you are spirit, and they are life." Was Jesus teaching us that if we do not drink His blood like vampires and eat His flesh like cannibals, we are missing spiritual reality and spiritual life itself? Let's explore this seemingly preposterous possibility.

How a Lamb from the Flock Pictures the Lamb of God

To better understand the sacrifice that provides eternal life, let's go back to the beginning of human history to discover why a sacrifice was needed and how it relates to the Eternal Lamb, Jesus.

20

Please stick with me through this difficult, but what I believe is a very important, section of the book.

The Adams' Family History

We will review three major events in the first family's story: first, Adam and Eve's loss of innocence; second, the acceptable sacrifice by Abel and the unacceptable one by Cain; and third, Cain's murder of Abel. As is usually assumed, was sin the primary issue in all three events?

The first event: After Adam and Eve ate of the tree of the knowledge of good and evil, they became aware of their nakedness (their loss of innocence) and were covered by shame. This is taught in Genesis as well as in Romans 5:12-19 where Paul taught that the fall of Adam, his loss of innocence, brought on all human sin. I agree, but many Christians have forced upon these texts an assumption that it was Adam's sin rather than his loss of innocence that was the primary focus in his "fall." You can search Genesis carefully and not find the word sin used when Adam and Eve ate of the tree of the knowledge of good and evil. This emphasis is a common Christian assumption.

I maintain it was loss of innocence that was portrayed in the Garden of Eden story. From the loss of innocence came Adam and Eve's shame and blame. Shame caused them to fear God and hide from Him. Adam then blamed Eve, Eve blamed the serpent, and both blamed God indirectly. After all, wasn't it God who made Eve for Adam and allowed the serpent to be in the garden? It was their loss of innocence that also caused Adam and Eve to see themselves as separated from God. God, however, sought them out, so the feeling of separation was based on their own marred thinking, not on God's action.

The penalty for eating from the tree of the knowledge of good and evil was that Adam and Eve would die. Obviously they did not physically die that day, so we can assume their deaths must have been spiritual. They died by seeing themselves as adults who could make a choice without God's involvement, and the resulting shame caused them to believe they were separated from Him. Their shame caused them to hide, and ever since, adult humans have tended to hide themselves from God out of fear or because of guilt.

It should be pointed out that in the Romans 5 text Paul says sin and death entered the world through the "transgression" of Adam, and then death spread to all humanity, for all have sinned. We should note that Paul *said* of Adam that he transgressed and had *caused* an offense. He even said that Adam disobeyed (God's instruction to not eat of the tree of the knowledge of good and evil). Paul never said that Adam or even Eve sinned; they transgressed. In other words, they offended and disobeyed. All of this language is based on the lowest level of offense toward God. This was not rebellion, because they were tricked by the serpent. This was not iniquity, and it was not blatant evil. It was, as in the definition of a transgression, an offense, a false step. Simply put, Adam failed to live up to his high calling as the image bearer of God. His offense was that he fell short of the high calling.

After Adam and Eve ate of the tree of the knowledge of good and evil, they lost their innocence and became aware of their nakedness, so God killed animals and provided their skins as clothing. In Genesis 3:21 we read, "Also for Adam and his wife the Lord God made tunics of skin and clothed them." We should notice that no mention was made of the blood, only the skin to cover their nakedness.

It is, therefore, possible that the original ceremonial sacrifice of an animal (in remembrance of the killing of an animal to cover Adam and Eve's nakedness) was not so much about forgiveness of sins (the shedding of blood) as it was about something else. Remember that God was also not pleased when Adam and Eve attempted to cover their nakedness with fig leaves. God rejected the leaves and killed an animal, not for the blood or for the meat, but for the skin! We do not know that the animal killed was a lamb, but it is most probable because soon after, God favored Abel's sacrifice of a lamb taken from his flock.

This brings us to the second event, the sacrifices of Cain and Able. Adam and Eve had two sons, Cain and Abel. Cain was apparently a gardener because he made a sacrifice to God of the best of his produce. Abel, on the other hand, sacrificed a lamb.

God was not satisfied with the offering of produce (which in no way provided an adequate covering for the loss of innocence), but found satisfaction with the offering of the slain lamb (a representation of the innocent One).

The first mention of sin comes in Genesis 4:6-7 where the text says, "So the Lord said to Cain, 'Why are you angry? And why has your countenance fallen?' (In other words, why are you pouting?) If you do well will you not be accepted? And if you do not do well, sin lies at your door. And its desire is for you, but you should rule over it." Up to this point Cain had not sinned. But he did not rule over the sin; it took control over him.

In the third family event, Cain sinned by killing his brother, Abel. It was almost as if he were saying, "You want an innocent sacrifice? I'll give you what you want!"

Many people struggle with God's apparent narrowness over the sacrifice of produce. They usually say it was because God wanted to keep the blood sacrifice before mankind as His only acceptable payment for sin. I know that later in history the blood shed was for the remission of sins, but I disagree with those who make it the primary issue in Genesis! The blood was not even mentioned at that time. I believe the taking on of the innocence of the sacrificed lamb is more important, even as it should be today. Why? Because it is the Lamb that brings us His innocent, sinless life, and with that life we find the power to stop sinning. The sin/forgiveness cycle never ends. We sin and ask forgiveness, only to sin again. It's true that His shed blood delivered us from the penalty of sin, but it is His body, the innocent Lamb, that delivers us from the power of sin by giving us His nature.

I want you to see that the ceremonial act of sacrificing an animal has deep spiritual meaning that cannot be fully portrayed by concentrating on the forgiveness of sin alone. Something much more important than simply the forgiveness of human sin was involved in the eternal story of the Lamb of God.

In all three events, I believe God was saying, not that way, but this way—not the product of your labor—gardening—Cain (or with Adam and Eve, not your own attempt to cover your nakedness with fig leaves), but the sacrifice of innocent life to cover your loss

23

of innocence, the lamb's lack of blame to cover your shame. This is the earliest lesson in grace—the receipt of life from another (a lamb) as a gift—a perfect picture of the coming sacrificial Lamb, Jesus.

The Lamb of God Was the Plan of God

The Bible declares that the Lamb of God was the plan of God before Adam and Eve were even created. Obviously, the fall of Adam and Eve, which destroyed the image of God in mankind, was seen and provided for before it happened. In the mind of God, the Lamb was already slain before God set the earth on its foundation. God had made the restoration of His image in mankind possible by providing Himself as the ultimate sacrifice. In this, God expressed the depth of His love and the sacrifice of Himself for others. To be created in His image means we have His nature, His self-sacrificing love, but this runs across the grain of the human self-preservation drive.

I believe that when Jesus prayed, "Thy will be done in earth, as it is in heaven" (Matthew 6:10 KJV), He was praying and instructing us to pray to be submitted to this sacrificial love above all else. Remember that the Creator God of the universe does not ask us to do what He does not do. He is love, and He always gives of Himself for the benefit of His entire creation.

Self-Sacrifice and Holy Communion

How can we better understand the spiritual significance and importance of self-sacrifice? I propose that we return to the objectionable topic of cannibalism and see how it relates to self-sacrifice and how that is portrayed in Holy Communion. First, let's review the average church communion service so we can see how the eating of Jesus' flesh applies. I am sure that the average Christian partakes of a wafer or little square of cracker and, because we have civilized and tamed the Lamb through our modern version of the communion service or Eucharist, never really thinks about what Jesus meant when He said, "This is My body, *broken* for you" (1 Corinthians 11:24).

It is almost certain that few realize His life had to be broken in order for us to participate in it, and our own lives must also be broken before Christ will manifest in us. Jesus wants to shock us into seeing the absolute need for total emersion of ourselves in Him, and He in us. We have, however, so sanitized His sacrifice that we do not see how the communion ceremony is like the ancient rites of cannibalism.

The Jews had witnessed, and sometimes even participated in, pagan worship where children were offered to their gods; and once roasted by fire, were thought to become the very body of the idol-god to whom they were sacrificed. But it was not simply the offering of children to the fire of sacrifice that they practiced; they also ate their roasted flesh so they might have the very character of the god they worshiped. In essence, in a spiritual sense this is exactly what we are doing as we partake of Jesus' flesh, the bread. We are spiritually eating the flesh of God to take on the character of God.

> **The proper effect of the Eucharist is the transformation of man into God.**
> **—St. Thomas Aquinas**

It's More About His Life and Glory and Less About My Forgiveness

In my entire Christian experience, having taken communion hundreds of times, I have never heard a pastor explain fully, to my satisfaction, what we were doing and why. Yes, they always said we were following the instructions of Jesus, who broke the bread from one loaf, but usually they did not explain the significance of eating His broken body. Jesus said, "Most assuredly, I say to you, unless you eat the flesh of the Son of Man and drink His blood, you have no life in you" (John 6:53). Paul repeated Christ's instructions in 1 Corinthians 11:23-30 and clearly said, "as often as we eat this bread and drink this cup we proclaim the Lord's death till He comes." I challenge all of us to see that it is an unworthy manner of participation in His death to see only our forgiveness of sins. We should examine ourselves to see if we have really feasted on His flesh in order that we might have His life and His character. After this presentation Paul instructed the "me first" participants at Corinth to stop fighting for more food and drink. Instead, they were to be willing to die to their rights, like Jesus, and become meek, sacrificing self for the sake of others and His kingdom.

The Story of Braveheart, an Indian Boy

Let me tell you a story that comes out of my family's interest in the American Indian culture, my father having been an archaeologist. Please don't confuse the name of the young Indian in my tale, Braveheart, with the movie by that name. My family story involves primitive worship and the innate drive of the human to try to understand the ultimate reality. In every human heart is the search for the Tremendous Mystery we all call God. We begin with the coming of age of a young Indian hunter.

Braveheart was only a teenager. He had practiced the ways of the hunter and had hunting instincts deeply ingrained in every gene. His great-grandfather, grandfather, and father were all honored by the tribe as hunters who provided for the food needs of the entire tribe. They had never before been without the provision of fresh meat. The provision would carry forward into the next generation only if the men of the hunting clan were able to pass the gift of fearless hunting on to every male in following generations.

Hunting skills could be practiced even in childhood. Now the day approached when Braveheart must become a man and have the heart as well as the hands of a hunter. Braveheart was so named because his family had great expectations that he would someday become the primary provider for the tribe. His great-grandfather had died, his grandfather was now crippled by arthritis, and his father had recently been severely wounded by a rogue grizzly bear that left him for dead after the attack. There had been a drought, and much of the wild game had left the tribal hunting lands in search of water and food. What few animals were left had become the primary food of the giant grizzly bear that was also dependent upon the game as a source of his food needs.

The tribe now became dependent upon young Braveheart, whose training in hunting was complete. However, he would be

26

honored by the tribe as the new provider only if he passed the ultimate test. He must kill the bear that terrorized the tribe and had driven them to the edge of starvation. His task was clear.

Braveheart had a problem. He was not brave, and he needed a heart change to become fearless in the face of this ultimate challenge. He knew that he could only prove himself by facing the bear, but he shook and became weak at the very thought of this daunting task. Children were crying from empty stomachs, and women were gossiping over the low probability that Braveheart could become their savior. The men of the village were as fearful as Braveheart because their training was not in warfare against a grizzly bear. It would not be long, they whispered, before this killer bear would begin raiding the village for fresh human meat. The entire tribe fell into deep depression.

Under a dark cloud of a foreboding, stormy sky, young Braveheart entered the deep forest that surrounded his village in the meadow. He knelt beneath a giant pine tree and said a prayer to the Great Spirit. He begged the Great Spirit for a new heart, for the courage to face the killer grizzly. Nothing happened. It was, as it had always been, as if the Great Spirit was busy in another forest and was not available for Braveheart. Anger began to swell up in his heart. Why was it necessary for him to face the killer bear all alone? Why did he not have the courage and bravery necessary in his own heart? Why was it that genetics and religiously practiced training alone were not enough to change him?

Suddenly he was aware of a stench of death in the air, and the crack of a twig breaking signaled the approach of his demon, the killer bear. He snapped to attention, and his muscles became as firm as steel. His body was suddenly soaked in sweat, and his heart pounded like it was about to explode. He breathed another prayer to the absent but deeply desired Great Spirit, asking, if it be possible, to let the bear move away from him. He also prayed that if he had to face the bear, the Great Spirit would give him the strength to fight as he had never fought before. Something like a wind chilled his body, and he trembled uncontrollably.

Taking an arrow from his quiver, he loaded his bow and waited. His arm muscles began to ache as he held the bow in

27

tension. The air was still. Suddenly, with unbelievable force and speed he saw the giant bear running at him, drooling over the thought of the easy meal he was about to enjoy. Braveheart waited, as the bear moved at lightning speed and was partially in midair about to pounce on him. With centuries of genetic talent, years of religious hunting training, and perhaps as much in total sickening dread as in any hunting skill, Braveheart let the arrow fly.

It struck the bear in the chest and entered the massive pounding heart. However, the bear was not going to be stopped by an arrow when its seven-hundred-pound body was in midflight. The bear's teeth entered Braveheart's extended arm. and its three-inch claws were on his back and at his throat. Braveheart collapsed in one broken heap.

So did the great bear. The arrow had been true, and its heart stopped pounding. Immediately the bear's frozen grip melted, and his teeth released the trap that held Braveheart's left arm. With all his strength Braveheart crawled from beneath the giant, now bloody carcass.

Centuries of instinct took over. With superhuman strength Braveheart rolled the bear on its side. Taking his hunting knife from its sheath he opened the bear's bleeding chest. Quickly he cut out the arrow-pierced heart and, raising it above his head, let the blood drip into his mouth. Then he took a giant bite, which he chewed and swallowed.

Braveheart came home with the grizzly bear's head on his shoulder and the partial heart in his hands. The entire tribe dropped to its knees in awe. Then they cheered, for he became a man that day—a brave-hearted hunter. The entire tribe feasted on bear meat. They danced and celebrated all night. But Braveheart was not to be seen among them. He had one last task to accomplish because he knew that he must never forget this experience. He found a log and, with the same hunting knife and his hatchet, he began to carve his own totem pole.

The next day the tribe was invited by Braveheart to join him in the sacred grove of trees where he had erected his totem pole. It represented many past generations of his ancestors, and at the top was a bear with a hole where the heart should be.

From that day forward the presence of the Great Spirit was easily found by Braveheart. All he needed to do was to look at the "totem-pole" bear and remember that he, Braveheart, now had the courage, strength, and very heart of a grizzly. Braveheart was never afraid again. He could look to the symbol and receive the life of a hunter, the very life of the great bear.

Moses and the Braveheart Story

In a similar but not identical way, Moses lifted up a serpent in the wilderness and all who looked to that brass serpent lived in spite of snake bites. Jesus was lifted up on His "totem pole"—we call it the Cross. All we must do is partake of His flesh and drink His blood symbolically, and we have His heart. This is what communion represents. It is that simple. It is that profound.

The point of the lesson of the Lamb is this—we can have more than the forgiveness of sins. We can have His very life! True, Jesus came to forgive us of our sins, but that is not the primary part of His sacrifice. The major point is that we can be united with Him in His death and raised in His resurrection. This provides us with much more than forgiveness. It provides us with His very life.

Jesus said that He had come to give us life of a different kind—loving, fearless, courageous eternal life that no longer is terrorized by Satan (the demon bear) and has no fear of death. We have the heart of Jesus if we want it. Do we really comprehend this?

Do you dare to challenge your own Christian traditions? Do you really want to be completely free? Do you want to get to know the real Jesus, the Living Lamb? I invite you to read on in the following chapters.

Interactive Discussion Questions

1. How do you personally react to the theme of this first chapter? What new things have you discovered about Jesus and how we receive His life?
2. Why might Christendom turn to the epistles, the letters of instruction to the church by Paul, and some others, as opposed to the Gospels, the stories of how Jesus lived? What would be the effect?
3. Why have we tried to lighten up the message of the Lamb of God?
4. Why would God design His eternal kingdom to rule through meek people?
5. How offensive was the text in John 6 to you? Had you really contemplated what Jesus was teaching and how His disciples felt? Why or why not?
6. Have you ever thought about the first appearance of the word *sin* in Genesis and recognized that the sacrifice of the Lamb was not primarily a sin sacrifice? Why do you suppose we always concentrate on our sins?
7. Why do you think that Jesus came to save us—primarily to forgive our sins or to give us new life? What difference would this distinction make?
8. How did you relate to the story of Braveheart? Do you see a connection between the totem-pole bear and the Savior, Jesus, on the cross? How are they different, and how are they similar?
9. When you look at the "totem pole" cross of Jesus, what exchange do you want to make in your life so that you are more like Him?
10. The next time you participate in communion, what will the ceremony mean to you? Might we be taking the elements in an "unworthy manner" if we do not feast on and become completely identified with Christ?
11. Is this exchange of life a reality for you?

Chapter 2
News Almost Too Good to Be True!
Jesus loves sinners

Meet Rita—Dancer and Mother

Rita (*not her real name*) entered my counseling office somewhat cautiously and with her eyes averted. She was a remarkably beautiful young woman and in great physical shape. She knew her sister had filled me in on her lifestyle, and I assumed that was the reason for her hesitation and shyness.

Shyness hardly seemed to fit with who she was. After all, Rita was a popular nude dancer in the big-city nightlife scene, but her demeanor in my office revealed she lived a double life. Sure enough, she was not only a nude dancer but also a devoted mother to her four-year-old son, Jason. While dancing was the way she made her living, Jason was all she lived for.

This young woman proceeded to tell me the gut-wrenching story of her life. She had been a runaway who came to Denver to escape the sexual and physical abuse dished out by her father. She had made it on the streets as a prostitute since she was 16. Now she was 29 going on 50, but her deep psychological and spiritual wounds had not yet marred her beautiful face and body. When we met, her only self-respect came from the good money she made by using her body.

Why, I asked, was she dancing and how did she feel about it? When Rita recognized that I didn't condemn her for what she did for a living, she started to relax and share her story with me. Dancing, she claimed, was the best job she could get. She had a baby-sitter each evening, and while little Jason slept, she earned more money per hour than most career women.

Rita had given up prostitution when she entered the nude-dancing scene. This did not mean, however, that she had given up men and sex. She was always watching the club participants, looking, she said, for the man she hoped might love her for more than her body. She often slept with one guy or another because it was better than spending the nights all alone.

During her earlier and more careless days, she had been pregnant several times and always had an abortion. About five years ago she found she was pregnant again, but this time something deep inside made her reconsider. She decided to go to a church to pray for direction. For the first time in her life, she said, she felt near to God and thought of Jesus and His mother, Mary. Mary had given birth to Jesus and was not married—so why couldn't she have a baby too? She had no idea of the price she had just committed to pay.

Within three months she was showing enough to have to take a break from her job—pregnant women don't make good nude dancers. Her meager savings lasted for the next ten months, and then she was financially pressured into going back to dancing.

Gradually, though, after the birth of Jason, her sexual life had all but disappeared. It wasn't that she was less needy or lonely, but she didn't want the growing boy to find some strange guy in the apartment with his mom—he was now old enough to ask questions.

Love Evades Her

As each year passed, she still hadn't found the man who would love her, make her happy, and be a candidate for daddy to Jason. Feeling somewhat hopeless, she now committed the problem to Jesus in prayer, asking Him to make her life complete. She was certain that God had spoken to her regarding the birth of Jason and that Jesus had given her comfort when she prayed, asking for a husband for her and father for Jason. She decided to attend a singles function in a church. It was there that she met David. He was handsome and obviously a believer, given his ease with the church environment. They talked, and he asked her to a movie and dinner.

It had been a long time since she had felt anything for a man, but her hopes and hormones combined, and by the end of that evening she wanted David to love her. She invited him up to her apartment after dinner. David began to ask questions about her life and this very young man, Jason, who lived with her. She confessed that Jason was her son and she had never been married.

David began to ask more questions. Rita assumed that a Christian who loved the Lord would be a caring, loving person, and she also hoped that Jesus had answered her prayers, so she began to share about her past life, including drugs, alcohol, and men. David became very animated and demanding. He asked her what she did for a living now.

When she told him the truth, he called her a slut and stormed out of the apartment. Rita collapsed into a tear-drenched heap, consumed with self-hatred and depression at a level she had not known since her withdrawal from crack and alcohol. The next morning she called her sister who referred her to me.

Jesus Forgives but Could a Man Forgive Her?

I asked Rita if she had asked Jesus for forgiveness of her sins, and she said yes. She said she even felt free in His love. The problem now, however, was whether any other man could ever love and understand her. She also had other questions—how would she be able to reenter the work force in another career and support her son if she had to remain single and had no high-school diploma? Why were Christians so judgmental when they didn't even take the time to know her?

With tear-filled eyes Rita asked me if God had truly forgiven all her sins even though she was still trapped in a less than holy life. "I love Jesus so much for forgiving me," she cried, and then she said, "I just can't seem to get this Christian life thing together." Now I ask you, what would you have said to Rita? Does she have eternal life in spite of her struggles with her lifestyle? Is it possible that the good news of the gospel of Jesus is that good? What can we learn from His life that could help us answer this question?

**The way Jesus lived and the good news
He proclaimed are identical;
He lived what He taught!**

How Good Does the Good News Have to Be in Order to Be Gospel News?

Perhaps no word in Christianity is better known than the word *gospel*. It means "good news." Certainly all of Christendom believes that Jesus brought us good news indeed, and most of us know there could be no gospel without Jesus' not only teaching it to us but also making it possible.

In our era, most daily news reports are filled with bad news. However, the kindly old reporter who loves to share "the rest of the story," Paul Harvey, has made a career of reporting good news. Yet, while his stories warm the heart, they fall far short of what the biblical Greek word *gospel* would characterize as good news. Why?

Only Spectacular News Can Be Great Enough to Be Called Gospel

We will better understand the power of the gospel concept if we define the Greek word. It is a compound word, *euaggelizo,* which means "good news announced by a special messenger." The concept is that the message must be spectacular. Examples of gospel-level news would include the coronation of a new king, the birth of a new prince, or the final victory in a war.

The second concept that defines *gospel* is the uniqueness of the messenger. Often the messenger was an angel sent by God or a herald sent by the king. A gospel messenger had an appointment by royalty or a mission from God to spread the good news to everyone.

In the context of the New Testament, however, there is a third element of the good news—it is a message from the heavenly kingdom. The good news of the gospel is sovereign news. It's an announcement of what the King has done for us. Notice the kingdom connection in Mark 1:14-15: "Now after John was put in prison, Jesus came to Galilee, preaching the gospel of the kingdom of God, and saying, 'The time is fulfilled, and the kingdom of God is at hand. Repent, and believe the gospel.'"

The gospel is spectacular news about God's love for people, presented as a gift from the sovereign King by specially appointed heralds. Properly given, it should be received with great joy.

The Modern Christian Gospel Is Often Less Than Spectacular Good News

Unfortunately, most modern Christians cannot define, let alone effectively communicate, the gospel in a way that the unchurched and unbelievers would rejoice over it. In fact, we often do such a bad job that they feel devalued by our gospel presentation. This would hardly qualify as good news. My premise is that we should tell the greatest love story ever like it is Paul Harvey's "the rest of the story." We often focus on trying to manage the sin of those around us rather than sharing the spectacular news from the King of the kingdom of heaven. The gospel is all about Him, and only about us in that we are its recipients. The biblical gospel is good news—period; not good news only if we are successful in changing our sinful lives into lives of perfect, holy living.

Making It New

To make matters much worse, we tell the gospel story as if our listeners were still shepherds from ancient Israel. In other words, we don't know how to use updated stories and examples from today's culture to explain scriptural gospel principles. Let me pose a question to you. How would you explain the gospel to today's postmodern people without explaining about blood, sacrifices, and sheep? Please understand, I am not devaluing these precious biblical truths about the blood of Jesus. I am asking if it might be possible to communicate biblical salvation without treating our contemporaries like first-century uneducated sinners? I certainly hope so!

It is my firm belief that the "old story" is ever new in each generation if we tell it like Jesus told it. To help us contextualize the gospel, consider this question: How would Jesus communicate the gospel message to the person on the street in our cities today? Would He tell about animal sacrifices and shedding of blood?

I believe the answer to effective gospel contextualization lies in contrasting the life of Jesus to that of the Jewish leaders in His era. In this way we should be able to discover the Jesus answer to the question of sharing the first-century gospel with twenty-first-century people.

The Central Message of the Gospel

The answer He gave was a way of living with absolute love, not a set of rules or doctrines to be adhered to. It centered in changing the image of God from a demanding ruler to a loving father. It also centered in the forgiving heart of the Father and not demands of perfect, sinless living. This is indeed good news!

First-century religious leadership was ineffective, but Jesus found sinners running to Him because of the power of His message. Let's take a look at the practices of the Jewish leaders of the Bible, the disqualified messengers. How did they live in light of their religious beliefs and convictions?

- They lived separate from normal people whom they called sinners.
- They created more and more laws and rules in their attempt to control people.
- They were proud of their bloodline, heritage, and traditions, and rejected others.
- They believed they were privileged people in God's sight.
- They wanted to be seen and respected.
- They felt justified in causing injury and death to vindicate their cause.
- They ruled over the people, making common Jews servants in their religion.
- They condemned rather than liberated people.
- They actually blocked people from relating to God.
- They grew rich at others' expense.
- They were dead spiritually.

Do We See Ourselves in the above List?

How about Jesus? How was He different?

- He lived with and loved average people, even notorious sinners.
- He reduced all law into two simple ones: Love God and love your neighbor.

- He claimed that being Abraham's seed was not so special, that even stones could become replacements if God wanted to change them.
- He taught that in God's sight the privileged people were to be servants of the poor.
- He wanted people who were rejected by society to be seen and respected.
- He had so much love that He healed even some of His enemies.
- He ruled only by truth and love and sought freed slaves to reign in His kingdom.
- He condemned only the self-righteous religious leaders and affirmed all others.
- He encouraged sinners to see that God their Father had open arms of love.
- He became poor that others might be rich.
- He was so spiritually alive that others saw and were attracted to God, His Father.

Do you see that His lifestyle and teaching were different from those of the religious leaders of His time and, unfortunately, common thinking of today?

Deciphering the Deeper Meaning

Jesus related the kingdom of heaven (God) to the gospel in Mark 1:14-15, "Now after John was put in prison, Jesus came to Galilee, preaching the gospel of the kingdom of God, and saying, 'The time is fulfilled, and the kingdom of God is at hand. Repent, and believe the gospel.'"

What can we decipher about defining the gospel from this text? Our first hint as to how to really define the gospel like Jesus did (and probably would today if He were here) is that it has something to do with being ruled over by God in His kingdom. This is known as the sovereignty of God. We American citizens can hardly relate. After all, we take pride in being free. No one rules over us in our democracy, or so we think. We are led to believe that the "good news" depends on our vote in its favor!

37

Our second hint is that the repentance Jesus demanded in the Mark text was related to "believing the gospel." We probably react to the word *repent* in the text with an immediate thought about repenting of our sins. Maybe this is included in the thought, but the kind of repentance referred to in this passage involved "the gospel of the kingdom of God." I believe that something new and different from repentance of sins is being indicated here. It is a change from an old to a new way of thinking and living.

The Gospel Is a Message of Pure Grace

Under the law mankind had to work hard to please God and hope for His favor. Under the new agreement mankind didn't need to work to please God but instead was asked to have faith in the favor God placed on all mankind. God's love is entirely unconditional, and this makes it universal.

Our third hint about the good news from Jesus is that it is not the religious leadership or the authority of the church that grants these benefits. Nor is it the will of human beings that brings about the benefits of the gospel. God is the source, and God makes the application by His will. Anyone who is the recipient of such wonderful grace is empowered and anointed to tell the whole world about the goodness of our God.

To summarize these three hints, we find that the good news (the gospel) Jesus taught and lived must include the method, message, and messenger:

1. The method of participation—the gospel delivers people from religious control because it is entirely something God has done for us. This makes God the absolute sovereign in granting kingdom membership and benefits.
2. The message of the gospel calls for our repentance for assuming a role in receiving God's favor. This kind of repentance means seeing this truth not just with human eyesight alone but also with spiritual sight. The glorious vision is that God is no longer angry at humanity. Paul said it this way, "God was in Christ reconciling the world unto Himself, not imputing [counting] their trespasses [sins] to them" (2 Corinthians 5:19).

38

3. The messengers of the gospel are those who have been overjoyed with the fabulous news. They need little encouragement to share because they are so excited that you cannot quiet them. This is what it means to be spiritually anointed as a herald of the King.

Jesus Promised Much More Than John the Baptist

Another way to understand this gospel of the kingdom message would be to contrast the message of John the Baptist, as a forerunner of Jesus, to the message of Jesus the King. In the message of John the Baptist we find these phrases:

- Matthew 3:2–"repent for the kingdom of heaven is at hand."
- Matthew 3:6–"confessing their sins"
- Mark 1:3–"preparing the way of the Lord"
- Mark 1:8–words about water versus spirit baptism
- Luke 3:3–"a baptism of repentance for the *remission* of sins"
- Luke 3:8–"bear fruit worthy of repentance"

For those people who had not yet seen and heard Jesus, there was a call to repentance and confession of sins. Luke clearly combined these into one thought — the "baptism of repentance for the *remission* of sins." The responding Jewish people were confessing and thinking about washing away their sins in preparation for the coming of the Messiah. In general, they had no knowledge that Jesus of Nazareth was the long-awaited King.

The *remission* of sins and having *sins taken away* are two very different things. In the Old Testament the sinner confessed his sin and offered a blood sacrifice to remove the guilt of that one particular sin. The next sinful failure by that person demanded another confession and remission. In this the baptism of John and blood sacrifices in the temple were alike. These acts could not take sins away but simply granted remission and covered them one at a time. However, John knew that the work of Jesus would accomplish much more. For this reason he cried out with great excitement when Jesus appeared at the Jordan River:

- John 1:29—"Behold the Lamb of God who *takes away* the sins of the world!"

How is this different from John's baptism? Let's contrast and define the difference in the two words that described their ministries. We will look at the quality of the forgiveness and the quantity of sins that were affected:

As to the Quality of Forgiveness:

John's baptism and ministry (the confession and repentance of sins) brought remission: in *Strong's Concordance,* word number 859, "remission," *aphesis,* means "freedom from sin, pardon, forgiveness." Remission applied to individual sins confessed at one specific time. However, Jesus once and for all eradicated sin at His death. The Greek word *airo* means "to take away." (See Strong's word number 142, "takes away," *airo,* means "lifts up, takes away, to lift and carry away.")

Airo, taking away, refers to all sins for all time, as explained in Hebrews 10:14, "For by one offering He has perfected forever those who are being sanctified."

As to the Quantity of Forgiveness:

John's remission related to one baptized *individual* dipped into the water. Jesus' "taking away" applies to the *world*—removing sins from people forever.

Who was the originator of the first baptism by water? Obviously, it was John the Baptist who first baptized those who came to him. Read Matthew 3:11: "I [John] indeed baptize you with water unto repentance, but He who is coming after me is mightier than I, whose sandals I am not worthy to carry, He will baptize you with the Holy Spirit and fire."

Who was the source of the second baptism, the baptism of the Spirit? John taught that it was Jesus who would baptize with the Spirit and with fire. In Scripture all those who are a part of the body of Christ were baptized at one time in the past. We read about this in Romans 6:3, "Or do you not know that as many of us as were baptized into Christ Jesus were baptized into His death?" Now this is indeed mysterious.

The Mystery of Total and Eternal Forgiveness

If we were baptized, or "placed into Jesus at His death," then God applied this death of our sinful nature about two thousand years ago! We certainly did not make it happen by believing the good news in our lifetime. We find that according to Romans 6:4, "Therefore we were buried with Him through baptism into death, that just as Christ was raised from the dead by the glory of the Father, even so we also should walk in newness of life."

How do we live a completely different kind of life, free from the penalty and power of sin? It is not simply by believing or by obedience of the law. It is by living a Christ-empowered life, walking by faith. Notice that the verse says *were* buried with Him. This is past tense and shows that the action of burial with Christ has already happened. The last phrase is present tense. In other words, by knowledge of the death and resurrection of Christ, and by knowing that we also died and were raised with Him, "even so we also should walk in newness of life."

We also know that the baptism mentioned in Romans 6:4 cannot refer to a physical water baptism, such as the physical baptism of John the Baptist. It also cannot refer to a physical baptism by our church either. This baptism, or emersion, into Christ, happened before we were born! Therefore, it cannot be physical but must have been spiritual. This is possible because spiritual things are not limited by time and space.

How does this teaching apply to the concept of a kingdom? Plainly, we cannot make something happen two thousand years in the past. It is therefore true that God made this happen and granted its privileges to us as a sovereign gift of His grace. Do you want further evidence for this two-thousand-year-old action? You will find it in Ephesians 2:4-6 where we read, "But God, who is rich in mercy, because of His great love with which He loved us, even when we were dead in trespasses, made us alive together with Christ [by grace you have been saved], and raised us up together, and made us sit together in the heavenly places in Christ Jesus."

It is obvious the only time Christ was "made alive" was at His resurrection. Again, this was about two thousand years ago. If we were spiritually made alive together with Him, we must assume that this happened without our will being involved. Do you see

41

how this makes God sovereign in the kingdom of heaven? How do we get into this new kingdom? Read Luke 12:32, "Do not fear, little flock, for it is your Father's good pleasure to *give* you the kingdom." Salvation and entrance into the kingdom are both free gifts granted to us without regard to our works or even our belief of certain doctrines.

John also taught this plainly in John 1:12-13, "But as many as receive Him, to them He gave the right to become children of God, to those who believe on His name; who were born, not of blood, nor of the will of the flesh, nor of the will of man, but of God." So how does this truth about the sovereignty of God impact the sharing of the gospel, the good news about what God has done for us?

Jesus Rejected Pharisaical Religion

In the kingdom of Jewish religion, Pharisees, Sadducees, and Scribes ruled. They promised entrance into God's favor by obedience to the Ten Commandments and a multitude of other rules and rituals. They were the gatekeepers and extracted a heavy price for their favor. Jews of that era had to work for their desired reward of God's favor, and that favor was as short lived as the time between the most recent sin and the next they would commit in the future. This created a permanent need for the favor and assistance of the religious leadership.

The Jewish leaders had no power over people except as it applied to the law. By expanding and defining the law in detail, they were able to keep people in bondage to service and sacrifice. Even when some of the people lived near-perfect lives, it only led to self-righteous pride. All the law ever brings us is guilt and pride—guilt if we don't obey the law and pride if we do.

Freedom in the Kingdom of Heaven

In the kingdom of God (also known as the kingdom of heaven), Christ rules over mankind on God's behalf and freely offers forgiveness to everyone. The heavy weight of laws and rituals is replaced with a light burden: only one two-directional law—the law of love. Our new Ruler, our heavenly King, Jesus, changes our hearts to become more loving, and His Spirit within us empowers loving behavior. In this way Jesus now rules over us as a servant who took away *all our sins*—past, present and future. The sins are forgiven and remembered no more, and are no longer the prime issue.

He then empowers us by His Spirit to become more and more like Him—ones who love. Our loving is now the most important thing. In John 13:34 Jesus gave us His commandment, "A new commandment I give you that you love one another, as I have loved you, that you shall also love one another." Jesus taught further, saying, "By this shall all men know that you are my disciples, if you love one another."

The "Kingdom of the Church" Misleads Many

Unfortunately, too often in the "kingdom of the church" today the leaders and their laws rule over people, just like the religious leaders and their rules did in Jesus' day. In these churches, members are often promised God's favor only if they obey the Ten Commandments and a multitude of other rules and rituals uniquely selected by their specific denominations. Their religious leaders are the gatekeepers, and they extract a heavy price for their favor. Often, members are considered "good Christians" if they attend every service, teach, sing in the choir, are prayer warriors, have disciplined devotional times, etc., and especially if they tithe. Giving to the church is so emphasized that sometimes sinful behavior is even overlooked if the sinners are heavy givers. All of these are "good" things, but without love, according to Scripture, they are "filthy rags" of self-righteousness.

We are told that salvation is a free gift of God's grace, but often the implication is that we have to work for the reward of God's favor. Like the Jews of old, today's Christians feel their acceptance in Christ is short-lived—lasting only until the next sin. Then they are afraid they have fallen from His grace and are back under condemnation.

Any terrible struggle with addictions, emotional bondage from past abuse, a messy divorce, or (heaven forbid) homosexual behavior, and suddenly the free gift is torn from their clutching

43

fingers with threats of church excommunication, being labeled a sinner, losing their salvation, being damned to hell, or in some cases accused of never having had real salvation in the first place. I cannot see how life in some modern churches has improved much over the Pharisaical rule in A.D. 30.

But, you may be thinking, *My church isn't like this*! Wonderful, I hope that is true. I know there are some "kingdom of heaven" churches. Unfortunately, they are all too few. And, unfortunately, there are even fewer "kingdom of heaven" Christians, even in those good churches.

Not me, you may be saying! Well, maybe me, too is more appropriate. For application of the principles of gracious living, answer these questions:

1. Do you see your freedom in Christ primarily as freedom *from* something or *for* something?
2. Is your salvation mostly seen as forgiveness from sins or is it seen as empowerment to live a brand-new loving life? Jesus said in John 10:10, "I have come that they may have life and that they may have it more abundantly."

May I be so bold as to say:

- If your primary view of Jesus is mostly as Savior (One who took away your sins so that you may some day get into heaven), then you may well have been contaminated with a low-grade gospel message.

- If you also struggle over whether or not your confession of sins was complete and sincere enough to have you covered, then you may well have believed a low-grade gospel message.

- If you believe that affirmation of a set of doctrines brings salvation, then you have believed a contaminated low-grade gospel message.

- If you think that Jesus came primarily to forgive our sins and not to give us a brand-new kind of life, then you have believed a contaminated low-grade gospel message.

- If you think that your entrance into the kingdom of heaven is up to you and your changed behavior, then you are *really* contaminated with a low-grade gospel message.
- If you condemn certain people because of their education, skin color, behavior, addictions, or flaws, then you have embraced a contaminated low-grade gospel message.
- If you often say that certain people can't be real Christians because of their church affiliation (doctrinal beliefs) or their continuation in certain sins and failures, then you have accepted a contaminated low-grade gospel message.
- If you believe that the only real Christians are active, committed members of a church, then you have accepted a contaminated low-grade gospel message.

I suggest that we take the words of Jesus very seriously. He presented a simple and unconditional version of forgiveness and God's favor to mankind. Read His challenge of the religious leaders of His day, and then I will rephrase this challenge to make it applicable to the present culture. Matthew 21:31 states, "Assuredly, I say to you that tax collectors and harlots enter the kingdom of God before you."

Judge Not Who Is and Who Is Not a Member of the Kingdom of Heaven

We do not have such a low view of tax collectors in our society. We joke about our dislike of IRS agents, but for a different reason. The tax collector of Jesus' day was a traitor to Israel. He worked for the Roman rulers. He used his authority to charge more than the taxes due to Rome and then kept the difference. In this way the tax collector was abusing power.

What of the harlot? She was one who also used men. She charged for sexual favors. In many ways she was powerless in society but used the power of lust to make her living. Both of these categories of people were despised and hated by the righteous Jews.

Tax-Collectors, Harlots, Liars, Thieves, Sinners, and Other Chosen Friends of Jesus

Not so with Jesus—He openly loved and accepted them. We see no evidence that He first demanded change before He would befriend them. The result of His love was that many changed their behavior, but He did not expect them to stop sinning before He would love and accept them. For this reason they believed that God the Father loved them unconditionally. They could see the love of God in the eyes of Jesus.

Now we can make a modern-day comparison. I believe that today Jesus would say that prostitutes, drug addicts, petty thieves, new-age followers, and homosexuals are entering the kingdom of God before us, the religious folks. Why? Because they know they need the love of Jesus, and many believe that God has already forgiven them, even when they are trapped in their sin. Do you seek further proof of Jesus' acceptance of sinners?

Jesus and the Prostitute

There is a great story about a sinful woman, undoubtedly a prostitute, who came to a party given for Jesus. Well, we assume it was for Jesus, but perhaps the host held the party for his own benefit. We read in Luke 7:36-50 about this party host, Simon the Pharisee, who asked Jesus to come to dinner. The story is so filled with the gospel truth that I have chosen to include it here in its entirety for your review, followed by comments about what I see in this powerful text.

"Then one of the Pharisees asked Him to eat with him. And He went to the Pharisee's house, and sat down to eat. And behold a woman in the city who was a sinner, when she knew that Jesus sat at the table in the Pharisee's house, brought an alabaster flask of fragrant oil, and she stood at His feet behind Him weeping: and she began to wash His feet with her tears, and wiped them with the hair of her head; and she kissed His feet and anointed them with the fragrant oil.

Now when the Pharisee who had invited Him saw this, he spoke to himself, saying, "This man, if He were a prophet,

46

would know who and what manner of woman is touching Him, for she is a sinner."

And Jesus answered and said to him, "Simon, I have something to say to you."

And he said, "Teacher say it."

There was a certain creditor who had two debtors. One owed five hundred denarii and the other fifty. And when they had nothing with which to repay, he gladly forgave them both. Tell Me, therefore, which of them will love Him more?"

Simon answered and said, "I suppose the one whom He forgave more." And He said to him, "You have rightly judged."

Then He turned to the woman and said to Simon, "Do you see this woman? I entered your house; and you gave Me no water for My feet, but she has washed My feet with her tears and wiped them with the hair of her head. You gave Me no kiss, but this woman has not ceased to kiss My feet since the time I came in. You did not anoint My head with oil, but this woman has anointed My feet with fragrant oil. Therefore I say to you, her sins which were many are forgiven, for she loved much. But to whom little is forgiven, the same loves little."

And He said to her, "Your sins are forgiven."

And those who sat at the table with Him began to say to themselves, "Who is this who even forgives sins?"

Then He said to the woman, "Your faith has saved you. Go in peace."

Just a few observations are in order. These will surprise you if you do not fully understand the grace of God:

1. The act of love shown to Jesus by this prostitute is shocking. This kind of intimacy was not shown in public.
2. Pharisees see the exterior person but cannot see the heart attitude.
3. Jesus points out that sinners know they need Him and love Him for His unconditional acceptance.
4. The emotion-filled question, "Do you see this woman?" must be noted. First of all, women were like children, often

overlooked and not seen. Secondly, Simon cannot see that the prostitute is really a child loved by the Father. Would we join Simon in condemning her? We have no right to judge what Christ has set above condemnation.

5. The reason she is forgiven, saved from her sins, and told to go in peace is not what we would expect. She made no statement of faith. She did not affirm any salvation doctrines. She did not get baptized. She simply "loved much." Hear it again as Jesus said it, "her sins which were many are forgiven for she loved much."

Do you see the illustration of the good news, the gospel? People are forgiven because they love God so much for loving them when they are undeserving. Are you that free in the message of the gospel of grace? So, once again, what would you tell Rita?

Interactive Discussion Questions

1. How do you feel about Rita?
2. Would you tell her she must stop dancing for money?
3. What is our responsibility as Christians to people who, like Rita, are trapped in an unacceptable behavior?
4. If we know God judges the heart and not the actions, what might be God's judgment of Rita?
5. Would you welcome Rita into your church just as she is? Why or why not?
6. How does it offend your concept of salvation that Jesus said, "Her sins which were many are forgiven because she loved much?"
7. Who else that you know might be forgiven simply because they love God?
8. How are you acting toward the unchurched and non-religious people who claim to love God in spite of their unacceptable behavior?
9. How do you think the religious establishment today presents the gospel message?
10. Do you believe that today's version of the gospel is wonderful enough to qualify for the gospel good news?
11. What might God require as repentance if repenting of a specific sin is not the issue?
12. Are you more concerned for religious sin management in our society or for the freedom of pure grace that only requires love?

Notes:

Chapter 3
Get Free From the Burden of Truth
Jesus and the truth

What is the truth? Jesus said in John 8:32, "You shall know the truth, and the truth shall make you free." Obviously this is an important issue for followers of Jesus, but what exactly is truth?

Before we begin a review of the Gospels and what this statement might mean, I believe we must return to the crucifixion story and review the interaction between Jesus and Pilate. Read John 18:35b-38a—Pilate asked, "'What have You done?' Jesus answered, 'My kingdom is not of this world. If My kingdom were of this world, My servants would fight, so that I should not be delivered to the Jews; but now My kingdom is not from here.' Pilate therefore said to Him, 'Are you a king then?' Jesus answered, 'You say rightly that I am a king. For this cause I was born, and for this cause I am come into this world, that I should bear witness to the truth. Everyone who is of the truth hears My voice.' Pilate said to Him, 'What is truth?'"

Does Truth Matter?

Absolute truth is unknowable for finite human beings. We only know the truth we can observe, and our observations and perceptions are always limited and biased. Nevertheless, many Christians tend to insist that our truth is the only ultimate truth.

Truth is the basis of peace, friendship, and unity, but also war, enmity, and division. Our perception of truth either binds us together in unity with others who agree with us or causes us to divide and separate from those who see things differently. For example, both American patriots and Muslim fundamentalists in our day are committed to their own truth, even to the point of death. Of course, truth matters immensely.

Usually our personal concept of reality is what we call the truth. That truth, therefore, changes as our perceptions change. I have found that human perceptions of reality and truth on a worldwide basis have also changed over time with the progression of science, and my own personal perceptions have changed as I

51

matured in age and experience. I, therefore, believe that what we claim as truth evolves.

The Evolution of Truth

Let us rethink this illusive subject we call the truth. The fact is that while pure truth is unchanging, our understanding of truth is constantly changing. For example:

- In the 1100s mankind believed that alchemy could change lead into gold.
- In the 1300s mankind believed that the Earth was the center of the solar system.
- In the 1400s mankind believed that the Earth was flat, not round.
- In the 1800s mankind believed that manned flight was impossible.
- In the 1940s mankind believed that nuclear radiation was harmless.
- In the 1950s mankind believed that death or crippling were inevitable from polio.
- Today we believe that...????

  The knowledge of the truth is very illusive. The famous German playwright Gotthold Lessing said,

  "If God held all truth concealed in his right hand, and in his left hand the persistence for striving for the truth...and should say, "Choose!" I should humbly bow before his left hand and say, Father, give me striving. For pure truth is for thee alone." (from *Eine Duplik*, 1778)

  Mesmer, the noted doctor of hypnotism, wisely wrote, "Truth is nothing but a path traced between errors." The wasteland of Error is far greater than the narrow path of Truth that runs through it, and mankind is forever wandering off into it. (*What Mesmer Believed*, Reprinted from The Journal of the National Council for Psychotherapists and Hypnotherapy Register, Summer 94.

We can rightly say that the search for God is the search for ultimate reality—the search for truth. It is a continuing search because we find that the truth, especially about God, is an inexhaustible subject. We also know that our own ability to understand truth is limited and constantly changing. This is especially true in regard to our religion. Think about the changing view of truth you have had in your own experience.

My experience unfolded like this:

- I first believed that our little church had the true message from God and that others were in error.
- Then I believed that some other churches had an even better grasp on biblical truth than my own.
- I was sure that anyone who drank alcohol was going to hell.
- I believed that Southern Baptists who grew tobacco were obviously sinful.
- I was certain that those dreadful Catholics were obviously going to hell.
- I believed that black people were cursed and whites must not marry them.
- I believed that Charismatics and Pentecostals were influenced by the devil in their emotionalism.
- I was certain that liberal theologians had nothing of value to say to me.
- I was concerned Billy Graham might be a liberal because he shared his pulpit with Methodists.

My Personal Discoveries About Truth

I have come to realize that what I believe is in process and always contains some error. A crushing of my ego and an admission of my limitations preceded my own personal journey of belief so that I might have less security in life now, but greater humility. I also found that my past concept about truth's being the basis of my security was deceptive, proven by the fact that I always had to defend my perceptions of truth with great vigor lest I be forced to admit my error. I finally realized I did not have faith in the truth, but faith in my level of commitment to what I believed to be true.

Nevertheless, Jesus said, "You shall know the truth, and the truth shall make you free." For me, my freedom is constantly growing as Jesus progressively leads me to deeper and deeper levels of spiritual reality. My faith now rests in the spiritual journey I am taking and in the presence of Jesus as we travel toward ultimate truth—the knowledge of God. I am more satisfied with the journey and less focused on my goal of trying to determine what the truth should be. It is more about experiencing God and less about defending my doctrinal concept of the truth.

It is like climbing a mountain where, with my arrival at every peak, I am convinced that I have arrived at the top only to find that there before me looms another higher point. Each false summit seems like the top, but the actual summit is much higher and hidden in the clouds. However, I am now more content with the view from each peak and not so proud of conquering the whole mountain.

A good example of this spiritual-truth journey in the Christian community is the study of doctrine. It often leads to a concentration on one lower mountain peak when, in actuality, that is just a false summit. But do not take me wrong. I love doctrine. I have simply found that it often left me dry and reveling in my successful completion of the lower summit at the expense of following Jesus onward and upward. How about you?

Stages of Psychological Development (Maturity Levels) Affect Our Perception of Truth

As humans, we mature through a number of well-documented psychological stages, each with its own level of understanding of our world. Social scientists are finding that the whole of mankind is also maturing slowly to higher levels of understanding.

Erroneous Truth and Childish Thinking

The apostle Paul spoke of the transitions in our conception of truth when he instructed the believers in Corinth to put away childish things. By this he meant that our truth concepts are usually faulty at the beginning of the faith journey. Let me further illustrate the human maturity levels of our perception of truth. All of the known levels can be reviewed from the eight-stage brief description on the next few pages.

54

One simple example is that as children, we are often very strong in our defense of how we see truth. Try to explain to a young child that it was fair for his brother to take the bigger piece of cake because he is older and bigger. The child sees this as simply unfair and cannot begin to understand the cognitive and reasonable argument. He only feels cheated. I remember the television comedian Lily Tomlin playing the role of a child sitting in that oversized rocking chair with her doll. She would explain her version of the facts to an adult voice and complete her statement with, "and that's the truth!" Obviously it wasn't.

Within our societies we find that the version of what is true reflects our own age and the maturity of our peer group as well. For example, you might be a very mature individual who lives in a society of people that reflects an early stage of development. You know that you do not fit within your society. On the other hand, you might be a very young or somewhat immature individual living in a society of intellectual and scientific giants. Again, you would not reflect your society.

This is what makes the concept of truth so difficult. Jesus, obviously, was spiritually and psychologically much more mature than the Jewish nation into which He was born. He was way beyond the level of Pilate, even though Pilate was His superior in the political and military realm, and I believe He remains far superior to our Christian leadership and religious experience in this day. Although we might have superior scientific knowledge compared to Jesus', if He were to reappear with only His Jewish training of two thousand years ago, we would still not have spiritual knowledge superior to His. We find then that what we claim as truth varies with our own maturity and the maturity of our culture. The claims of Jesus are designed to speak to us at any age and maturity, and in any culture. This is what makes Jesus a universally recognized spiritual master.

Higher Levels of Understanding of Spiritual Realities Free Us from Immature Thinking

Jesus said He is the truth, that His truth will make us free, and that His kingdom is a truth not of this world. From this we might project that when Jesus taught about spiritual truth, it was truth from His spiritual-kingdom perspective.

He taught about a reality that is not normally seen or entered. He presented truth from the unseen spiritual realm. I invite you to review your own level of spiritual and psychological reality. If you do not know where you are on this mountain journey, you can hardly discover your own level of truth perception.

A complete book could be written on the subject of human perception of truth. It is, therefore, not my purpose to completely define the truth pilgrimage in this chapter. Let it suffice to review what many others have taught and learned about human perceptions.

Following I present a brief description of the eight stages of psychological development (which are also progressive levels of consciousness) and how they affect our individual perceptions of human truth—our reality—and how we understand the world around us, as it applies to understanding the source of life:*

1. Womb Stage—Mom and I are one.

Before birth we cannot be certain that the embryo has consciousness as we would usually describe it. The embryo draws life from the mother and cannot distinguish self from mother. There is, however, a sense of unity that would dictate consciousness that the source and self are one and the same.

2. Baby Stage—Mom is my source.

After birth the unity experienced in the womb is replaced by the consciousness that the little self is disconnected, and the baby cries out for food and warmth. The baby instinctively searches for the breast in order to receive milk. The baby slowly develops a consciousness that mom is separate from self, and mom becomes a primary "other" being in the baby's mind.

3. Child Stage—Daddy is my source.

As the child develops and is weaned, the food supply is no longer found in a direct connection to the mother through nursing. The child becomes aware there is another "other" (Daddy) who brings home the food from hunting or by working. I know that today a woman may bring home the food as well, so in that case the first other (mother) and the second other (father) would be one and the same person. The shift of consciousness would not be a change of focus on a person but, instead, a change of role by that person.

4. Teen Stage—I become my own source.

Normal progression in human development brings a desire to become an individual who can be independent, working or hunting for his or her own food. Pride naturally develops if the teen is able to produce its own food, shelter, and clothing, and this makes the person conscious that he is his own source of the necessities of life. This stage of development is both necessary and dangerous. Too little independence creates a teen who cannot be an individual self, and too much independence often creates a teen who thinks that he or she needs no one else. The result of dependent living is poor self-esteem or self-image, while the result of independent living is a self-focus that causes pride and rebellion. We call this form of self-image an egotistic person.

5. Worker/Warrior Stage—My leader is my source.

For most people, the consciousness and focus gradually change from self alone to the person in relationship to the leader who may be the boss, the king, or the general. The leader is depended on to provide the job, the security of citizenship, or the battle plan. Thus, the source of life becomes the leader.

6. Citizen Stage—My nation is my source.

The consciousness next focuses on a broader perspective. It is not my boss, my king, or my general alone that is the source of life. The person begins to think much more inclusively, and the nation or ethnic clan is seen as the source of life. This is the source of patriotism and of military commitment to one's nation that calls for the sacrifice of life for the benefit of the national cause.

7. Wounded Healer Stage—God is my source.

A person's national consciousness is shattered when that person is wounded in battle and finds that the self, the leader, and the nation are all inadequate sources of life. The focus moves beyond all of these to a transcendent God who must be the source of all things. In the woundedness of defeat, one becomes conscious of the inadequacy of all other previous perceptions of the sources of life. This means that Mom, Dad, self, career, the general, and life itself become inadequate, and one is forced to search for the source behind all other sources. The person then begins to cry out for God. Jesus put it this way in Luke 14:26: "If anyone comes to Me and does not hate [meaning choose against] his father and mother, wife and children, brothers and sisters, yes, and his own life also, he cannot be My disciple."

8. Wise Old Sage Stage—God, the Source and I are one.

In the advanced stage of life, the stage the apostle John called the "fathers" of faith, the person returns to the earliest level of consciousness, the embryonic stage. In this stage a growing sense of oneness and unity with God the Source replaces the feeling of being separated from God, that many express has been a lifelong battle for them to overcome. This is especially true for those who struggle with an overcoming sin or for those who are prideful and sense no need for God in their lives. Peace reigns in the person's life as he or she realizes and is enlightened to see that God was never separate from the self. The apostle Paul put it this way in Acts 17:28, "In Him we live and move and have our being." Thus the progression of consciousness, the spiritual perceptions, cycles back to the beginning, to understanding the True Source and our eternal relationship to Him.

The Oneness with God that I am describing is not the oneness generally proclaimed by the New Age Movement. They tend to dwarf God's divinity and to enthrone man as his own God. It is true, however, that we were created in that image and likeness of God and the work of Christ restored and even improved the image within mankind. Nevertheless, our differences from God are much greater than our likenesses to Him.*

* Note: For the scholar, in the back of this book you will find a detailed note about the uniqueness and limitations of this oneness. There is also a chart that presents the stages of human development and perception as they correlate with history. It shows that mankind in general is experiencing a progression of consciousness. This progression also relates to biblical progressive revelation, meaning that Old Testament saints knew less about God and His plan involving Jesus Christ than did the New Testament saints.

Conceptualization of the Human Enemy

In a similar way we change the way we see our source and the way we see our enemy, the one who keeps us from receiving from the Source. This time I will present the concept of truth about the enemy of mankind, not in the individual's conception but in four past historic eras:

First Century—Church versus Rome
Political warfare

The first century Jews and Christians would have believed that the Roman Empire was their enemy and that it stood between them and God. This was especially true when Caesars burned Christians as torches to light their gardens and had many thrown into the arena to be eaten alive by lions.

Medieval—Church versus demons and despots
Spiritual warfare

During the medieval era Christians would have believed that wicked rulers and demonic forces were their enemies and that they stood between them and God. At that time the church began to demonize its enemies and claim that the church was in a battle to establish the church's kingdom on earth, the kingdom called Christendom.

Modern—Church versus science
Rational warfare

For much of the modern era following the Enlightenment, Christians falsely believed that science was their enemy and that it was attempting to separate them from faith in God. Consequently, they demonized science and, at least initially, rejected many scientific advances. For example, Christians opposed the use of electricity on the basis that the unknown power might be demonic. And we all know how the church has battled against any teaching of evolution on the grounds that it is a godless theory.

Postmodern—Spirituality versus materialism
New-reality warfare
We are now entering a postmodern era, and Christians are reacting negatively to it because they cannot believe there might be a reality greater than the modern era, mechanical, law-controlled reality they have been taught to accept as absolute truth. They want certainty, and they do not understand that the postmodern people are much more comfortable with mystery.

In reality, the enemy was never so much political, demonic, rationalistic, or new-reality based. The greatest enemy to discovering truth is our selves, our stubborn clinging to a limited view of truth that keeps us from continuing our personal journeys into deeper truth and true spirituality. We need to let go of our self-limiting truth claims and accept the nature of our truth journeys—a continuous reevaluation of what we believe to be the truth. What is one primary force that keeps us from progressing in our consciousness of the truth? Down through time truth has gone through a painfully slow metamorphosis, often because of peer pressure.

Tribalism Versus Truth
Truth may be very hard to accept when it causes us to grow beyond our peers. We all need to belong, but at what cost? Ancient people could not survive alone. Mankind ruled over his environment only by forming tribes that worked and fought together. In order to keep peace within the tribe, the group formed a powerful system of bonding around certain accepted behaviors. These were called taboos. In essence, the tribal leader said that you could belong only if you agreed to obey the tribe's rules. If you broke a taboo, the result would be death or forced separation from the tribe. There is still a form of tribalism active in humanity, and it is also found within the Christian religion. When truth controls us,

however, we are not controlled by the pressures of our tribe or peer group.

Indoctrination Is to Taboos as Education Is to Freedom

For the last three hundred years Christians generally have not been educated—we have been indoctrinated. We are indoctrinated not to think deeply but to accept by faith the teaching of our leaders and the taboos that result. Taboos are a forced belief structure, but truth is what sets us free even from ourselves. At first we do not even dare to test our own beliefs. We are led like sheep and are controlled by powerful taboos against any questioning of church authority. We usually want to fit into our tribe or Christian peer group and be accepted by them more than we want to discover truth.

We often blindly accept authority without asking the obvious question, which authority? Why is my church right and so many others wrong? If I had been born into another denomination or religious tribe, would I not be just as certain about their doctrines? Who is the ultimate authority?

Thomas Watson, a fifteenth-century philosopher, said, "Whoever fears to submit any question to the test of free discussion loves his own opinion more than truth." (Christian Quoting.Org)

We must be open to discuss our differences if we are to move beyond simplified, traditional taboos.

What Difference Does This Make?

Truth must be accepted; our traditions must not control us. The truth always glorifies Christ and His Father, our God; traditions always tend to glorify man. We may, in fact, worship our doctrine of salvation from sin at the expense of worshiping the source, God. Ask yourself, which gives Christ greater glory, His being the human Savior, or being the Lord of life? We are eternally grateful for His redemption, but we must be careful to understand that being saved from our sins is not as important as our having real life and becoming like Him. The search for truth is the search for God who is the source of reality and all truth.

61

I found that my historical tribe, evangelical fundamental Christianity, had so indoctrinated me that I struggled with finding and enjoying God. I found that I had to leave most of my preconceived ideas about God in order to find God. Did I want truth or traditions? My historic traditional truths and taboos gave me a false sense of security and a shallow knowledge of God.

If my search is not for truth and not for God, but for a belief system, I am reduced from a spiritual seeker to a worshiper of formulas that produce a sense of certainty.

Because we do not like to rethink things, we tend to prefer our idols and illusions to the ultimate reality that is filled with mystery and challenge. To understand my struggle with truth and certainty, and I suppose your struggle also, I want us to think how mankind has progressed in what it accepts as truth. Mankind's progression is also our usual individual perception of truth.

As Mankind Developed, the Definition of Truth Changed
- First only the truth you feel
- Then the truth you are told
- Next the truth that empowers you
- Recently, the truth that you can prove by reason
- Now to the truth you experience—perception versus senses

You will probably notice that human consciousness of truth and our personal growing up have definite parallels. Next we see how the definitions of truth parallel our stages of human maturity.

- The truth you feel   Child
- The truth you are told   Adolescent
- The truth that empowers you   Teen
- The truth that you can prove by reason   Adult
- The truth you experience—
  perception versus senses   Wise old person

Actually, we only know a fraction of any truth at any given stage. Only God could know all truth. Still, Jesus said that to know the truth is to be made free. How can we be made free from our opinions we have labeled as truth?

We defend our truth in order to be secure and right! Jesus said He is the truth. We know, however, that this claim does not mean that Jesus taught the definitive truth about non-spiritual concepts: He was not the truth of mathematics; He was not the truth of science; He was not the truth even of theology.

How, then, is He the truth? In what way did He expose ultimate truth? I propose that He is the truth of the kingdom of heaven (God) reality. We find His truth in His kingdom, His life, His gifts, and His transcendent reality.

Our Changing Reality and the Development of Our Truth

This search for truth has been addressed by Jesus and many others. What have others said about the search for truth?

Francis Bacon "Certainly, it is heaven upon earth, to have a man's mind move in charity, rest in providence, and turn upon the poles of truth." (Francis Bacon. 1561-1626. *Of Truth*.)

Protagoras, "Man is the measure of all things, of the existence of the things that are and the nonexistence of the things that are not." (*Protagoras on Truth*, G. J. Mattey, October 24, 2001)

Socrates, "Is this not roughly what he [Protagoras] means, that things are for me such as they appear to me, and for you such as they appear to you?" (*The works of Plato* (427-347),

At Any Given Time People Have Their Own Concept of Reality

Today people say we have a new way of thinking in postmodernism, and we call this relativism. Respect for the opinion of others is expected and called tolerance. Relativism and tolerance are the guiding principles of postmodernism, just as rationalism and absolutism were for the modern age. Relativism with tolerance is, however, not new; it is at least as old as Protagoras.

63

If truth is simply what we name and claim as our opinion, why not drop the search for truth altogether? Why not simply wallow in the plurality mud of conflicting perspectives and forget the concept of truth? After all, why search for the truth when truth threatens human peace? Conflicting claims of truth have been the basis of most of the hideous crimes against humanity. Was the Inquisition right? Were the Crusades right? Was Hitler right? Was Stalin right? Is Osama bin Laden right, or is George Bush right? The kaleidoscope of changing opinions labeled as truth continues to confuse and separate humans even to the point of war.

Within Christendom, fundamentalists respond radically to the panic over the plurality of opinions. Their response to the conflict about truth is often to irrationally affirm beliefs that most people cannot accept. The revulsion of fear Christian fundamentalists feel (when told there may not be an absolute truth behind our security claims about God) leads them to claim all the more loudly that the Bible must be read and accepted as literal truth. Therefore, Christian fundamentalism does not willingly enter the journey of discovery of truth because such a search in and of itself would threaten the claim that they already have "the truth."

One result, for example, is that they battle over the twenty-four-hour day creation theory, because in the fundamentalist perception of truth every chink in the armor must be defended lest the whole protection and security system fail. Believing themselves to be defending the truth, they accept the statement in Genesis that each creation day ended with an evening and started with a morning as proof that each day was twenty-four hours long.

This is rationally unacceptable, however, when the same scripture (Genesis 1:14) also says that the lights in the firmament of the heavens that divided the day and the night were not made until the fourth day. We can see then that fundamentalists sometimes argue for their interpretation of truth and favor their opinion over the actual search for truth.

A Fundamentalist is a Fundamentalist No Matter Where We Find Him

Fundamentalism is not limited to the Christian religion. Radical fundamentalists in Islam justify the killing of innocent people in order to advance their claims to their truth. So also the Inquisition leaders, the Crusader soldiers, and, in our era, Stalin and Hitler. From this I believe we can conclude that fundamentalism is primarily an intolerant philosophy of life that insists on dividing everything into truth or error, black or white. To put this dichotomist view of life into biblical terms, it is a return to "the tree of the knowledge of good and evil. When we insist on always dividing everything into categories of black or white, it only leads to death. The alternative is to eat of the Tree of Life, which means that we are willing to accept the paradoxical mysteries of life and the mysteries that our reality actually presents to us.

In our era the concepts of modernism with its prejudice toward absolute rationalism resulted in intolerance, while the rapidly advancing society of postmodernism with its openness to mystery is much more tolerant and questioning.

Our Western culture inherited modernism from the Enlightenment of the seventeenth and eighteenth centuries. The modern mind-set placed an emphasis on the superiority of reason (rationalism) and the necessity of technical proof of truth along with an emphasis on human autonomy (individualism). Author Brian McLaren said, "our modern age has predisposed us to a limited range of postures with the Bible. It's all objective analysis and forensic science, always trying to prove something. It's all about a kind of aggressive analysis of the text, reducing it to something explainable by our preconceptions, turning it into moralisms or principles or outlines or conclusions or proofs or whatever." (*Precis & Critique of A New Kind of Christian* by Brian McLaren, Amy K Hall, 9/7/04)

Therefore I believe we can say modernism produced religion at the expense of true spirituality.

The current trend toward postmodernism is a trend away from rationalism and individualism, and toward living at peace with uncertainty and paradoxical mystery. The postmodern mind-set acknowledges that the universe is a scary and unpredictable place.

This new generation does not believe that the world is becoming a better and more organized and predictable place. The postmodern thinker recognizes the advance of human ingenuity but does not believe that every problem will be solved. This leads to a realism and skepticism about any absolute-truth claim.

Today truth is seen as a quest, not an artificial scientific or logical formula. Thus, I believe that postmodernism will lead toward an even more pluralistic view of spirituality and of the reality we all seek—the ultimate reality we call God. Unfolding forms of postmodern spirituality will be more mystical, more experiential, and less rational and pragmatic.

The Search for Truth Means Taking Some Risks

To embark upon the ultimate journey toward God (meaning toward truth and toward the ultimate reality), one must be willing to become set free from the safety harness of religion. You may have needed a safety harness to learn about mountain climbing, and you know you cannot venture beyond the harness without risk. You cannot have an exhilarating walk on the edge of the cliff on the journey of life as long as you stay in the training harness that is designed to catch you if you fall. Falling is necessary to taking a walk of freedom up that narrow cliff trail. What, you may be asking, is the training harness? I believe that it is the formulas of faith, the security of our doctrine, and the belief in the necessity of absolute, knowable truth.

A safety harness may have served you well in learning the techniques of mountain climbing. You will not, however, have the thrill of adventure unless you take the risk of falling. The harness has no place in your eventual upward ascent. In a similar way your rationalism eventually defeats your attempts at becoming rational, because we cannot prove the unprovable, we cannot define the indefinable, and we cannot construct any theology that does not have some internal conflicts of logic. Cut off that harness! God can only be reached at the end of the mountain-climbing journey when you walk without all that protective gear.

Jesus invites you on a never-ending journey into the spiritual realm of ultimate reality. If you are holding on to the security harness with one hand and grasping for the tremendous thrill of stepping out into an unknown spirituality on the other hand, let go of the security harness. Falling from your security is not such a great threat to your spiritual life as never venturing out into the quest for truth, the quest for the experience of walking with Jesus into wonder and mystery.

Freedom to Fail and to Fall Is Necessary to Fellowship with Christ

So, what does all of this have to do with Jesus the Christ? What might His claim to be the truth and the life (the ultimate level of reality) have to do with directing today's postmodern thinkers on their journeys toward truth? How might you and I embark on this quest for truth led by Jesus? I believe the simple instructions for this faith journey into real spirituality are contained in the quotation by Francis Bacon offered earlier: "Certainly, it is heaven upon earth, to have a man's mind move in charity, rest in providence, and turn upon the poles of truth."

How might Francis Bacon have found this trinity of action in the teachings of Jesus?

- **Principle One—If it isn't loving, don't do it!**
  Jesus said it simply in John 15:12-13: "This is My commandment, that you love one another as I have loved you. Greater love has no one than this, than to lay down one's life for his friends."
- **Principle Two—If you can't trust it, don't rest on it.**
  Jesus taught this simply in Matthew 6:26: "Look at the birds of the air, for they neither sow nor reap nor gather into barns; yet your heavenly Father feeds them. Are you not of more value than they?"
- **Principle Three—If it isn't freeing, don't believe it.**
  Jesus also taught this very simply in John 8:32—"You shall know the truth, and the truth shall make you free."

These three principles are the entrance keys to His kingdom—Love, trust, and be free!

This is the simple formula that led Jesus to say in Matthew 19:14, "Let the little children come to me; and do not forbid them, for of such is the kingdom of heaven."

But please do not deduce that I am saying this freedom gives any of us the freedom to simply do as we please. That freedom would prove to be a false freedom in that it would place us back under bondage to sin, to self, and/or to egocentricity. This is not true freedom. Biblical freedom is not, however, a principle. It is a person. Jesus said, "If the Son makes you free you shall be free, indeed." John 8:36. It is His life, His Spirit, and His nature in us that brings true freedom.

And lest you think that entrance into the ultimate reality, the spiritual kingdom of heaven, is difficult and only obtained by a select few, remember that Jesus also said in Luke 12:32, "Do not fear, little flock, for it is your Father's good pleasure to give you the kingdom."

When Jesus faced death by crucifixion, Pilate asked Him, "What is truth?" Let me be so simple as to state that the truth according to Jesus is this:

Jesus answered, "My kingdom is not of this world. If My kingdom were of this world, My servants would fight, so I should not be delivered to the Jews, but now My kingdom is not from here." Pilate therefore said to Him, "Are you a king then?" Jesus answered, "You say rightly that I am a king. For this cause I was born, and for this cause I have come into the world, that I should bear witness to the truth. Everyone who is of the truth hears My voice." Pilate said to Him, "What is truth?" And when he had said this, he went out again to the Jews and said to them, "I find no fault in Him at all." (John 18:36-38)

In summary, we can apply the three entrance principles to the teaching of Jesus just before He gave His life for mankind.

- **First, the whole life of Jesus was loving**. His very purpose for coming into this world was to give His life for His sheep, those

68

who would trust in Him. Jesus met the *love* requirement of the kingdom. This was no sentimental love; it was the highest form of agape and compassion, the love of God by which one gives his life for others.

- **Second, the whole life of Jesus demonstrated absolute trust.** Jesus could not have faced the horror of the Cross without first having given His will over to His Father. In the garden He prayed, "Nevertheless not My will, but Yours, be done" (Luke 22:42). In this, Jesus demonstrates for us that we can face any life event with a confidence that trusts God with whatever is out of our control.

- **Third, the whole life of Jesus was given for the cause of truth that makes men free.** I would say that anyone who lives with love and trust has the highest form of freedom. Yes, we know that His sacrifice freed us from the penalty of sin, but there is much more. You can be set free from yourself and, like Jesus, you can live in such freedom that this world and all its trials cannot keep you from perfect peace. Even facing death, we can say with ancient Job, "Though He [God] slay me, yet will I trust Him" (13:15)
.

Let me encourage you to consider that no matter what you believe:
- If you are not consistently living out of a sacrificial love for God and others, you have not yet fully entered into the kingdom of heaven.
- If you are not fully trusting God in all life's trials, looking for the good He has promised even in your worst situations, you have not yet fully entered into the kingdom of heaven.
- If you are not so free that you are free from your self, so free that you can live lovingly without any concern for rules and rituals, you have not yet fully entered into the kingdom of heaven.

Paul said it this way in 1 Corinthians 13:13, "And now abide faith, hope, love, these three; but the greatest of these is love." In this Paul would be in agreement with Francis Bacon, "move in charity, rest in providence, and turn upon the poles of truth."

Love, Trust, and Be Free in the Truth.

- Faith is trusting God's providence (His control) using even what is evil for our good.
- Hope is the freedom to keep searching for God and truth in a sick and twisted world.
- Love is living for God and others in such a way that you find you can truly love yourself.

Jesus was decidedly more concerned that you and I live in love, trust, and freedom in the truth than that we confirm our belief in biblical doctrines. The test is not what we believe but how we live. Do we really meet this test? Do we rule over life out of our spiritual resources?

Finally, I want to explain that vital Christianity understands that the biblical word *believe* means "to trust." The truth of the kingdom, the spiritual realm that Jesus proclaimed, is found when we absolutely trust Him to indwell us by faith and intimately join us in the mountain ascent. The recently passed era of modernism has produced a Christianity that has generally reduced the biblical mandate to believe into a "statement of faith"— a set of doctrines we must believe. In so doing, it has caused many of us to miss the excitement of a trusting faith journey into the unseen spiritual realm of the kingdom of God. Are you less content now with your past spiritual progress than before we took these steps of understanding? Are you ready for another adventure up the mountain called spiritual truth?

Interactive Discussion Questions

1. Give some examples of how human conception of truth has evolved over time. (We have already discussed the flat earth and earth as the center of the universe theories, which have been replaced. Give others.)
2. What examples can you share of how your concept of truth changed as you aged and matured?
3. Does this mean that truth actually changed? If not, what has changed?
4. Why do you suppose the average Christian freezes at the Worker/Warrior stage of faith or concept of truth?
5. Mesmer's quotation, "Truth is nothing but a path traced between errors," suggests that finding truth comes only from first embracing some errors. Do you think this is true? If so, name some errors you embraced, and explain how they led to a different understanding of truth.
6. In the transition from rational warfare to new-reality warfare, modernists conflict with postmodernists. How do young people today tend to express their desire for a new experiential reality more than for doctrinal proof structures?
7. How comfortable are you with the uncertainty of reality?
8. Name some ways that Christians might deny reality in the search for certainty?
9. Do you feel that your Christian training was primarily indoctrination rather than education? What has been the result of this kind of training?
10. If biblical fundamentalism is less than one hundred years old and Christian evangelicalism can only be traced back to the eighteenth century, what might have caused these changes in the truth concepts of Christendom from the years of Christendom preceding them?

Notes:

Chapter 4
Jesus Throws a Party for Sinners
Jesus the friend of sinners

The life and ministry of Jesus revealed in the Gospels is a life of extreme contrasts when seen through His communication styles; how He related to various groups of people, as well as to certain individuals. How could this Man aggressively drive the money-changers and sellers of animals for sacrifice out of the temple with a whip and then passively allow the most brutal soldiers to whip Him and nail Him to a cross while praying that His heavenly Father would forgive them?

Jesus, Always Meek and Mild?

How could Jesus treat a notorious prostitute with gentle respect and claim she was forgiven of her many sins and then resort to name-calling when confronted by the religious leadership? He was, obviously, no Mr. Rogers who spread peace and happiness wherever He went. What caused this dichotomy?

May I be so bold as to ask, what if Jesus' primary message was much more about God's hatred of hypocrisy and abuse by the self-righteous religious leaders than it was about the awfulness of the sins of common people? I have been a Christian for over fifty years and have yet to find any pastor, church, denomination, or writer that places the emphasis on self-righteousness and not on sin. How about your experience?

Jesus, Friend of Sinner and Enemy of the Self-Righteous

If I am right, then the misplaced emphasis on people's sinfulness is the basis for legalism and the source of much spiritual abuse. Jesus, you see, came to set the record straight and to present His view of the heavenly Father as our Creator and Sustainer, our loving heavenly Daddy. At this point you are probably thinking, *but we cannot become so loving as to become soft on sin, right?* (I know this question arising from your emotions, because I had to deal with it in my own life)

73

Try this exercise: look for the words *sin(s)* and *sinner(s)* in the four Gospels, and see how these two words are used. Jesus used the label "sinner" to describe certain people, but He treated them with love and kindness. He also used this word to define the class of people who did not see themselves as righteous. Because He did not condemn them, they willingly became His friends and followers. He honored sinners by being their friend.

In John 5:14 and 8:11 we find the only recorded texts in all of the Gospels where Jesus ever told someone not to sin. Surprised? On the other hand, this same Jesus condemned the Pharisees, Sadducees, scribes, and religious leadership on many occasions. Listen to some of His choice words of condemnation for the religious leadership's self-righteous hypocrisy found in Matthew 23:13-29 (my paraphrase), "You shut up the kingdom of heaven against men,...your prayers are pretense because you steal from widows,...when you proselyte you make people like yourselves— sons of hell,...you are blind guides,...you are fools,...you tithe and make a big deal over it but you neglect justice, mercy and faith,...you clean up your outside but inside you are filthy,...you are like whitewashed tombs looking good but inside you are filled with dead men's bones and uncleanness,...you are sons of those who murdered the prophets,... Serpents, brood of vipers! How can you escape the condemnation of hell? Do you get the picture?"

Even in the two cases where Jesus warned about sin, there was a specific reason. First, in John 5:14 the man was infirm and could not walk for thirty-eight years. He did not know Jesus, did not confess his sin, and only had hope of being placed into the pool where he supposed an angel might heal him. Jesus simply spoke with authority and told him to take up his bed and walk. The message of authority overcame the message of bondage, and he was able to walk. Later, Jesus told him, "See, you have been made well. Sin no more, lest a worse thing come upon you." These are strange words indeed. If Jesus had been concerned for his eternal soul and was into modern-era evangelism, He might have said, "sin no more or you will end up in hell." But Jesus said, "sin no more," (John 5:14) so the man must have sinned in the past. Jesus seemed more concerned for his condition than his spiritual well-being because He did not forgive his sins. With all this in mind, what is this text about, anyway?

As a counselor, I know that most of the human conditions of sickness and infirmity are caused by psychosomatic sources, or at least are greatly influenced by the mind and emotions of the victim. The body often catches the soul's diseases. There are many forms of crippling caused by guilt. Jesus apparently knew this. In John 8:34-36 He said, "Most assuredly I say to you, whoever commits sin is the slave of sin. And a slave does not abide in the house forever, but a son abides forever. Therefore, if the Son makes you free, you shall be free indeed."

The story of the lame man at the pool of Bethesda illustrates how Jesus wants to set us free from slavery to sin. It does not deal with forgiveness of sins that we might attain eternal life in heaven.

Likewise, in John 8:11 we are dealing with the slavery to sin; in this case sexual desire. The woman involved had been caught in the act of adultery and was taken to the temple to be stoned by the spiritual leadership. The leadership tested Jesus by saying that the Law of Moses said to stone her. What did He say? If He agreed with the harshness of the law, He would not have been loved as the friend of sinners. If He sided with her and told them to leave her alone, He would have been seen as a breaker of the law. What He did was pure genius.

In verse 7 He said, "He who is without sin among you, let him throw a stone at her first." We know they all left because they knew they had sinned. Maybe some had never committed adultery, but which of them had even really obeyed the first commandment, "You shall have no other gods before Me"? They were self-righteous men, and the very essence of self-righteousness places self above God. This results in the sin of pride and the condemnation of others. No one in that unruly crowd was guiltless; all were sinners. The point Jesus is making is that self-righteousness, one-upmanship, is what keeps people from God, not their sins. According to Jesus, sinners know that they sin and need God, and this is the preface to receiving grace.

Did Jesus Warn the Woman So She Would Become Pure?

Jesus is careful to say, "'Has no one condemned you?' She said, 'No one Lord.' And Jesus said to her, 'Neither do I condemn you; go and sin no more.'" How quick we are to point out that Jesus told her to stop sinning. In our rush to judgment, we miss the lack of condemnation by Jesus. Why did He warn her against future sin? I believe that sexual sin such as adultery is addictive and, just as we have already seen, Jesus knew she was in bondage to that sin. Continued acts of adultery would have eventually led to her being stoned for sure. Any loving person would have warned her to change her behavior, but what about the startling statement, "Neither do I condemn you"? If Jesus was so dedicated to obedience to the Ten Commandments He would have had to point out to her that lawless behavior brings condemnation and eternal punishment—right?

No Condemnation of Sinners by Jesus

Jesus never condemned sinners because He understood how we are all trapped in one or another level of slavery to sin. Jesus was never self-righteous; He was always humble and gracious. He knew that sin was not as big a problem as the self-righteous religious beliefs we hold. These, not sin, are the greatest hindrance to our coming to God. Sin, you see, has its own bondage and misery, and will usually drive us back to repentance and to God. Not so of self-righteousness. If we have never committed sexual sins, for instance, we will probably be very quick to self-righteously condemn others who have. This attitude of self-righteousness is prideful, and pride stands between us and God.

The Justified Sinner and the Condemned "Saint"

In another gospel story Jesus taught about two men who went up to the temple to pray. We find them in Luke 18:10-14 and it is a very insightful story that supports my premise. "Two men went up to the temple to pray, one a Pharisee and one a tax-collector. The Pharisee stood and prayed thus with himself, 'God, I thank You that I am not like other men—extortionists, unjust, adulterers, or even as this tax collector. I fast twice a week, I give tithes of all that I possess.' And the tax-collector, standing afar off, would not as much as raise his eyes to heaven, but beat his breast, saying, 'God be merciful to me a sinner!' I tell you this man went down to his house justified rather than the other; for everyone who exalts himself will be abased, and he who humbles himself will be exalted."

Justification Before God Comes from Love and Humility

Apparently God is not impressed with tithing and fasting and is totally turned off by our pride and judgmental attitude toward others. Notice that Jesus never said the sinful tax-collector's sins were forgiven. He said the man went away justified, meaning just as if he had never sinned. In the mind of Jesus and under the laws of the kingdom of heaven, people are declared right before God based on their love and humility, not based on the purity of their lives.

Paul said it this way in Romans 4:5, "But to him who does not work but believes on Him who justified the ungodly, his faith is accounted for righteousness."

In Luke 7:47 we read, "Therefore I say to you, her sins, which are many, <u>are forgiven, for she loved much</u>. But to whom little is forgiven, the same loves little." (emphasis mine). This woman who was the subject of Jesus was humble and cried while stooping to love Him in front of the self-righteous judgment of the men like Simon the Pharisee. Her sins were forgiven because she loved much, and I might add, she humbled herself to serve Jesus.

This tax collector (the King James Version calls him a publican) was a sinner when he came up to the temple and a justified sinner when he went back to his house. He didn't even ask God to forgive his sins. He asked for mercy. He knew how much his life fell short of what God expected, and he simply asked God to be merciful to him as a sinner. His demeanor tells us he was humble before God. His prayer proved he was honest about his faults. He made no comparison of his life to others. He simply cast himself on the love and mercy of God, and as a result, he went away justified.

What Is Our God Concept?

Let me ask you to think about the concept each man had about God in Heaven. The Pharisee believed that God, like himself, was a strict demanding ruler who looked with condemnation on people when they sinned. For this reason Jesus said of the Pharisees in Matthew 23:4, "...For they bind heavy burdens, hard to bear, and lay them on men's shoulders, but they, themselves, will not move them with one of their fingers." Certainly the legalistic and demanding approach of the Pharisees was seen as condemnation for the people's sins.

The publican was a man who made his living by collecting taxes for the Roman government, laying a heavy burden on the people of Israel. Tax collectors were seen as traitors and extortionists because they worked for the hated Roman conquerors and made a profit by charging more taxes than they paid to Rome. I doubt that the publican stopped collecting taxes or gave up his job just because he was justified. Some followers of Jesus did return what they had taken, but no such statement is made about the publican in this story, nor does it appear to be a requirement for justification. Repentance and restoration are both good things, but they do not cause God to forgive us, and they do not bring about our justification.

God Forgives First and Looks for Our Repentance Later

What does it mean that he was justified as a humble sinner? The word *justified* means approved, accepted, and declared right by the judge. In our culture, we do not fully understand this word, but we do have a similar concept in today's political system. Our governors and president can grant a person freedom from the penalty of the law by setting aside a person's just sentence. We call this a pardon. This action removes the guilt and penalty, but it does not say the person was not guilty of breaking the law. The person is not condemned, but is nevertheless still a law breaker. This is the way God pardons us, the way He justifies us, and the way He has forgiven us.

To better understand God's role and our human responsibility in forgiveness, we need to understand God's character and our human condition. In our era, Christians tend to underestimate the love of God and overemphasize the need for human repentance. We often hear this error expressed in the claim that people must be repentant and hate their sins before they can be saved. This, however, is a wrong emphasis according to Scripture. Let's look at a few verses and apply their obvious face value, while not allowing our traditional view of sin and the sinner to warp the truth expressed in them.

Which Comes First, God's Forgiveness or Man's Repentance?

Romans 5:8—"But God demonstrates His own love toward us, in that while we were still sinners, Christ died for us."

Remember that while on the cross, Jesus said, "Father forgive them for they know not what they do." By definition, the forgiveness Christ asked the Father to extend is granted when we do not even understand the extent and horror of our sins.

Romans 4:5—"But to him who does not work but believes on Him who justifies the ungodly, his faith is accounted for righteousness."

In this text it is clear that justification comes when a person trusts the kindness of God. This trust is faith that causes a person to be declared righteous in God's sight.

What Leads Us to Repentance?

Romans 2:4—"Or do you despise the riches of His goodness, forbearance, and longsuffering, not knowing that the goodness of God leads you to repentance?"

Do you see the power in this verse? It is not fear of God or fear of punishment; it is not deep sorrow over our sins that saves us. It is not despising God—not thinking ill of His infinite love. It is His kindness, not His anger or wrath, that brings us to repentance.

What Kind of Repentance Is Necessary to Bring About Salvation?

Hebrews 6:1—"Therefore, leaving the discussion of the elementary principles of Christ, let us go on to perfection, not laying again the foundation of repentance from dead work."

In this text we can see why some might think it is speaking about repentance from sin, but the people described in this verse had been trusting in their works to please God. Their required repentance was to change their minds about what God required of them. God, also, requires nothing of us—not even repentance from our sins. God only requires that we repent, that we give up trying to do good works, and place our faith and trust in who He is, rather than trusting in anything we do.

Is God's Forgiveness Applied to People Only If They Repent of Their Sins?

Second Corinthians 5:18-19—"Now all things are of God, who has reconciled us to Himself through Jesus Christ, and has given us the ministry of reconciliation, that is, that God was in Christ reconciling the world to Himself, not imputing their trespasses to them, and has committed to us the word of reconciliation."

It is simply stated here. God has already forgiven all people (the world), and He no longer counts their sins against them. This is the good news we share in the ministry of reconciliation. We are already reconciled to God and totally forgiven by Him. We, however, have to believe it in order to benefit by it.

Mark 1:14-15—"Now after John was put in prison, Jesus came to Galilee, preaching the gospel of the kingdom of God, and saying, "The time is fulfilled, and the kingdom of God is at hand. Repent, and believe in the gospel."

Jesus clearly tied the gospel, the Good News, to repentance. But, this repentance is not simply repentance from sin or from our individual sins. I believe it clearly includes changing our minds about the way God reigns.

God, you see, does not cause us to feel guilty so that we will repent of our individual sins. Our own conscience and often other people do that. Satan, himself, is the accuser of the brethren. Instead, according to Romans 2:4 Paul taught, "Or do you despise the riches of His goodness, forbearance, and longsuffering, not knowing that the goodness of God leads you to repentance?" (emphasis mine). Thus God reigns in our hearts by His grace (unmerited favor) to us.

80

We submit to His reign over us when we get it through our stubborn heads that the Good News is based on a change of thinking, a new paradigm. God loves us more than He hates our sins. His love is triumphant, and He reigns in love.

How Broad Is the Forgiveness of God Appropriated Through the Death of Christ?

First Timothy 4:10—"For to this end we both labor and suffer reproach, because we trust in the living God, who is the Savior of all men, especially of those who believe."

Second Corinthians 5:19—"God was in Christ reconciling the world to Himself, not imputing their trespasses to them."

He forgives and loves us because that is who He is—the loving, forgiving God, and He has forgiven the whole world, all of mankind.

Which picture of God do you see when you think of your own or another's sin? Do you see the God of wrath who looks to punish offenders, or do you see the God of love waiting for our sins to cause us enough pain to drive us back to Him? Is God looking for perfect people or simply honest sinners who cry out for His mercy?

Jesus taught this contrast in the way mankind pictures God in one of His most loved parables, the story of the prodigal son, found in Luke 15:11-32. I want to make the following points about this story. First the context must be noted in 15:1-2, "Then all the tax collectors and the sinners drew near to Him to hear Him. And the Pharisees and the scribes murmured saying, 'This man receives sinners and eats with them'." We can see very plainly that this story is aimed at contrasting the separation and pride of the Pharisees from the reception and love of Jesus. Even the word *Pharisee* means one who is a separatist and excludes others from his level of religion. Jesus, you see, was into connecting, not separating.

The father pictured in the story Jesus told is the heavenly Father. He is very rich. He provides fairly for his children and even for his servants. There is no lack in His kingdom. Jesus illustrates the Father and His children by telling about two sons. The elder, we shall see, is like the self-righteous legalistic Pharisees. The

81

younger is much like the rest of us, simply an irresponsible lover of pleasure who seeks personal enjoyment more than the fellowship of his Father—at least at the beginning of the story. In Jewish culture the firstborn had a right to two-thirds of the estate of the father after the father's death, and the second son would have inherited one third of the estate. The younger son, being a pleasure seeker, demands his share immediately. To have taken the inheritance of the father before death was to wish the father dead in order that one could spend the money.

The father complies and gives the third to the younger son. He could have had him stoned because he just broke the commandment to honor thy father. He certainly could have had him whipped or lectured on being thankful. He did not. The father Jesus illustrates is a picture of our Father in heaven—One who loves us and gives us what we want, knowing that love and grace are more powerful than anger and law.

The young son spent all on prodigal living. The word *prodigal* means a spendthrift, not a sinner. The son simply acted as if there were no tomorrow and no reason to be frugal. Apparently he wanted pleasure and the admiration of people who attended his lavish parties more than he wanted to act in love. This caused him to run out of money, and then there was a famine in the land. He had to feed pigs and was so hungry that he felt the pigs were better fed than he. Eventually he came to himself—this means he got real.

He remembered that even servants in the kingdom of his father were better treated than pig farmer's servants, so he resolved to return to the father, acknowledging he had sinned. He did not believe he deserved to be treated like a son, only as a servant of the father.

Notice and rejoice in the attitude of the father, our Father. He was watching for the boy to return. He had saved the fatted calf for a celebration. He ran to the boy and kissed him. He gave him back a royal robe—restoring his sonship rights. He gave him the father's ring—much like extending the boy all of the father's credit. He fully restored him. As in the father's mind, in the mind of our heavenly Father, we were destined to come back. Sin was designed to drive us back home. The prodigal's and our return caused a great celebration.

Now we see the illustration of the wrong concept of God and the resulting miserable life in the story of the older son. He was still in the field working. He could not fellowship with and enjoy the father or the wealth, because he felt he must never stop working for the right to the family fortune. He never had a party. He was angry when there was a big celebration over his younger brother's return. He claimed that this rebel had spent the father's money on prostitutes—a telling point because there was never any mention of a harlot in the prodigal's wild parties. He was incensed that the fatted calf was wasted on the younger boy when he had never had a party with a goat dinner. He claimed he never had the opportunity to make merry. Whose mind-set was this?

The father, our Father, said, "Son, you are always with me, and all that I have is yours. It is right that we should make merry and be glad" (verses 31-32). Earlier (verses 4-7) when Jesus told the first of the three parables—the shepherd finding a lost sheep— there was rejoicing in heaven over the return of the sinner. I believe that sin's pain destines the return of the honest sinner. I believe that the Father in heaven knows this and expects the honest sinner to come home. I believe that the one group of people who never come home to the party are the ones who never leave home but remain in the field, working for what God has already given them. I believe that self-righteousness that judges the freedom of others is the biggest bar to blessings. I believe that both sons were always with the father in that they were accepted and loved by Him equally. It is only the wrong concept about God that prohibits both from remaining in and enjoying His blessings.

Can you celebrate your total acceptance by the God of heaven, and can you see that love and grace are much stronger than any sin? Can you see that Jesus did not condemn the younger son but did condemn the older for his foolishness in misjudging the love of his Father? Can you party in your freedom?

Perhaps the following verses will speak to you as they do to me. They are about God's acceptance of sinners in the new kingdom of heaven based on what Christ has done for us.

83

- Matthew 11:30—"For My yoke is easy and My burden is light."
- Romans 14:15—"I know and am convinced by the Lord Jesus that there is nothing unclean of itself; but to him who considers anything to be unclean, to him it is unclean."
- Romans 14:20— "Do not destroy the work of God for the sake of food. All things indeed are pure, but it is evil for the man who eats with offense."
- 1 Corinthians 6:12— "All things are lawful for me, but all things are not helpful. All things are lawful for me, but I will not be brought under the power of any."
- Titus 1:15—To the pure all things are pure, but to those who are defiled and unbelieving nothing is pure; and even their mind and consciences are defiled."

Interactive Discussion Questions

1. Chapter purpose—Modern evangelicalism still concentrates on people's sin and their need of forgiveness. Jesus did not say He had come to give us forgiveness of sins. He said He came to give us life! Sinners are trapped in guilt, but self-righteous people are trapped in pride. Jesus rarely lectured about sin or even condemned a sinner. He often railed against the legalistic Pharisees and their burden of self-righteous laws. Can we accept this? Why might we struggle against this?

2. How could this Man explode in anger and, with a whip, drive the money-changers and sellers of animals for sacrifice out of the temple and then allow even the most brutal soldiers to whip Him and nail Him to a cross while praying that His heavenly Father would forgive them?

3. Why did Jesus call the religious leaders names like sons of the devil and then accept notorious sinners?

4. If we are truly loving, does it mean we will be soft on sin?

5. Is God looking for perfect people or simply honest sinners who cry out for His mercy?

6. How do you see God—as a punitive, strict ruler or as a loving daddy? Why did you adopt this vision of God?

7. Why do you suppose the author let us know about the accusation against Jesus, "This man receives sinners and eats with them" before he told us Jesus' teaching on the prodigal son?

8. Is your life generally characterized by reception or by separation?

9. Do our churches generally act in receptive ways regarding sinners? What evidence do you see that supports your conclusion?

10. Are you more like the prodigal son or the older brother?

Notes:

Chapter 5
Religious Leaders May Be Thieves - Jesus
Jesus the shepherd king

Human beings are, as far as we know, the only creatures in all creation designed to bridge between the spiritual and physical realms. Angels are spirit beings only, animals are physical creatures only, but humans were designed to be fully physical beings while at the same time image-bearers for God, the ultimate Creator Spirit. In this, mankind is always being stretched to live simultaneously in two realms of reality: the kingdom of this world (the physical) and the kingdom of heaven (the spiritual).

Jesus, the perfect man, came to teach us how to live in the realms of the physical and spiritual concurrently. He modeled this new kind of humanity, humanity in humility, as the servant shepherd. The extreme test of His humility came through His being called to die for His sheep. In John 10:11 Jesus declared, "I am the good shepherd. The good shepherd gives His life for the sheep." Servanthood for Jesus meant giving up His life that His sheep might have a better life.

The Now Present Kingdom of Heaven

Jesus taught us the truth about the spiritual realm—the kingdom of heaven, and this is part of the message of the gospel. The really good news is that we do not have to wait until we get to heaven to enter the kingdom of heaven. As Christians we know that the kingdom of heaven is within us right now, co-resident with the indwelling King—Jesus Christ.

Believers, however, have at least two problems related to the kingdom of heaven, probably because we have been taught so little about it. First, most expect to enter the kingdom of heaven only at death and thereby miss the truth of the kingdom currently present with us. Secondly, we are apt to become proud of our kingdom-of-heaven status, thus defeating the potential benefits of a present-kingdom reality. Such an elevated state of being, as to live connected to the Creator and to express His very image, can easily lead us to pride. Therefore, Jesus taught that one must humble oneself and become as a child to even enter this spiritually present kingdom that exists with us and in us right now.

Entering the Kingdom Realm

We can enter the kingdom of heaven and begin living above the chaos of this present world, but only through humility. Strangely, this kingdom realm available to us now must be entered by a change of thinking, a new paradigm, a rebirth. We must again become as children. In Matthew 18:3-4 we read, "Assuredly, I say to you, unless you are converted and become as little children, you will by no means enter the kingdom of heaven. Therefore whoever humbles himself as this little child is the greatest in the kingdom of heaven."

In summary, we can say that because of these two problems, many do not attain the peace, power, and purpose that come with experiencing the kingdom of heaven as a present spiritual reality. When we become spiritually aware of our present life in the kingdom of heaven, we experience *peace,* because the kingdom of heaven is a reality that transcends earthly turmoil. As sons and daughters of the King, we are able to exercise spiritual *power* over the forces of evil present in this world. Our divine *purpose* is to advance the invincible kingdom on earth as the life of Jesus expressed through us changes our culture.

Earthly Rulers versus Servant Kingdom Leaders

This world's rulers and leaders often rule over others for their own benefit. They enjoy acting as masters and lords. They want recognition and praise. They want to be in control. Now listen to what Jesus taught about leadership from the perspective of the spiritual kingdom-of-heaven realm. We can read this teaching in Matthew 20:25b-28. "You know that the rulers of the Gentiles lord it over them, and those who are great exercise authority over them. Yet it shall not be so among you; but whoever desires to become great among you, let him be your servant. And whoever desires to be first among you, let him be your slave—just as the Son of Man did not come to be served, but to serve, and to give His life a ransom for many."

In this illustration we find that the absolute King of the heavenly kingdom reigns not from power or authority but from servanthood. He made Himself last that we might be first. He made Himself a slave that He might become the King of love. Love, therefore, is the power in the kingdom of heaven and in the realm of the spirit.

An Earthly Example of a Spiritual Principle

Let's now add to the overall picture by looking at the example of a person who, by following Jesus, lived in this world with the power, peace, and purpose that came from already being a part of the eternal spiritual kingdom of heaven.

Who was this servant shepherd that reigned from the kingdom of heaven in such a way that all the kings of this earth honored her? She was born August 26, 1910, in Skopje (now in Macedonia). Agnes Gonxha Bojaxhiu was the daughter of an Albanian grocer and his wife. She entered the Catholic ministry in her youth. The Loretto Sisters of Dublin sent her to Calcutta, India, in 1929. There she took the name Sister Teresa, after Saint Teresa of Lisieux, the patron of missionaries. She received the Nobel Peace Prize on December 13, 1979.

The recent Pope John XXIII recalled his own experience with the legendary nun: "I had many occasions to meet with her, and I have the vivid memory of her small figure, bent over by her past years of service among the poorest of the poor, but always full of inexhaustible interior energy: the energy of love of Christ."

"The example provided by Mother Teresa," the Pope said, "is one that all people should emulate; her witness was eloquent for everyone, believers and unbelievers alike, in that she was able to transform her love of God into a life of unselfish service to others. Her contemplation became love and her love became contemplation." (*Nobel Lectures, Peace* 1971-1980)

Mother Teresa's life was completely devoted to the poor and needy. Once when Pope Paul VI gave her a white Lincoln Continental, she auctioned the car and used the money to establish a colony for leprosy patients in West Bengal. Soon after Mother Teresa's death, <u>Pope John Paul II</u> beatified her, the latest step in the Macedonia-born nun's path to Catholic sainthood.

Simple Saint or Super Saint?

Was this unusual Catholic sister a super saint? No. She always claimed that she did nothing any other person could not do. She simply loved all people regardless of their belief or status just as she loved her Lord Jesus. She claimed that she ministered to her Lord when she ministered to the poorest of the poor.

Jesus obviously agreed with this principle of kingdom love. Here is what He taught on that subject in Matthew 25:34-36, 40, "Then the King will say to those on His right hand [the sheep] 'Come you blessed of My Father, inherit the kingdom prepared for you from the foundation of the world; for I was hungry and you gave Me food, I was thirsty and you gave Me drink, I was a stranger and you took Me in, I was naked and you clothed Me, I was sick and you visited Me, I was in prison and you came to Me.' Then the righteous shall answer Him saying, 'When did we....' And the King will answer and say to them, 'As much as you did it to the least of these My brethren, you did it to Me.'"

Can we not agree that Mother Teresa lived out the power of kingdom-of-heaven love, and in so doing, was honored by the leaders of this world? Let's read a few statements about life in her words:

- "In the West there is loneliness, which I call the leprosy of the West. In many ways it is worse than our poor in Calcutta."
- "There is a terrible hunger for love. We all experience that in our lives—the pain, the loneliness. We must have the courage to recognize it."
- "No matter who says what, you should accept it with a smile and do your own work." (Mother Teresa's Message To Fourth UN Woman's Conference)

90

I do not agree with the pope in his authorization of sainthood for Mother Teresa—I say she already was a saint—her life proved it. But the important point I want to make is that each of us as believers can live with this kind of compassionate love if we will humble ourselves and become as a servant to others. We may never match the quantity of her acts of love, but we may equal the quality by simply acting as a servant and showing compassion to others who are in need. The lonely in America are in many ways worse off than the poor of Calcutta in the estimation of Mother Teresa.

Jesus the Servant Shepherd

My question for us is this: what if we in today's churches were more interested in shepherding hurting and lost sheep than in building our own religious kingdoms? I am afraid that many of our present Christian leaders bear no resemblance to Jesus, the humble servant shepherd. Jesus, you see, still loves and has great concern for scattered sheep. In His day He spent His time with, and gave His life for, the "lost sheep" of Israel. He had very little time for the leaders of the religious establishment. If Jesus were to return today, He would probably see that most of Christendom has become greedy and self-centered. We have turned our focus to what we want and need and have shunned truly needy people. We avoid the hurting because their pain makes us uncomfortable; their questions go unanswered because we won't take the time to get involved.

Inside or Outside Focus?

If we have Jesus' compassion and His focus, will we not be more concerned for the lost sheep outside the "church with walls"? I believe that with His compassion and love we will have a kingdom focus on the scattered sheep who have no Shepherd rather than a focus on the existing church membership. Church focus often attempts to bring people to Jesus, but kingdom focus will bring Jesus to the people.

Hey Jesus, Where Do You Go to Church?

Jesus made His focus plain when He answered the question of the Samaritan woman in John 4. In her interaction with Jesus in verse 20 she asked Him, "Our fathers worshiped on this mountain, and you Jews say that in Jerusalem is the place where one aught to worship." In essence she was asking if holy places matter. Notice Jesus' answer: "Woman, believe Me, the hour is coming when you will neither on this mountain, nor in Jerusalem, worship the Father.... But the hour is coming, and now is, when the true worshippers will worship the Father in spirit and in truth; for the Father is seeking such to worship Him" (verses 21-23). It is entirely fair to deduce from this teaching that Jesus did not believe we need buildings to worship God.

Temples as Buildings or Bodies as Temples?

There is little documented evidence before the New Testament period for any synagogue in Israel being used as a dedicated religious building. When Jesus taught in the synagogues, these were not religious temples but small buildings with porches and outer patios. They served as schools, courts, libraries, and marketplaces during the week as well as Sabbath-day gathering places. There has been no dedicated synagogue found by archaeology from before the second century A.D. There was only one primary national temple in Jerusalem, and it was destroyed in A.D. 70. Long after this, local synagogues began to be built, having distinctly Greco-Roman architecture.

The Capernaum synagogue is thought to be the ruins of the earliest known dedicated building used for Jewish Sabbath meetings, and it was built in the third century. Certainly, after the life, death, and resurrection of Christ the place no longer matters because God's temple is not a building. Our very bodies are now the temple of the Holy Spirit. I believe this is why Jesus prophesied the destruction of the Temple in Jerusalem and why after that destruction all sacrifice for sin ceased. So where did the Christian emphasis on church buildings and temples come from?

There were no Christian church buildings before Constantine, the Roman emperor whose supposed conversion to Christ led to a state-sponsored temple building, not unlike the pagan temples of Rome. The early church met in homes. Acts 7:47-53 shows us that "the Most High does not dwell in temples made with hands." In Acts 20:20 Paul told us that, "...(I) taught you publicly and from house to house." According to archeological findings, no church buildings existed except a single house that had been remodeled to allow for more seating.

Even the Jews of Jesus' era did not worship in dedicated buildings but instead used public buildings built for other purposes. [See pg 556, Pictorial Encyclopedia of the Bible, Merrill C. Tenney, General Editor, "...the basic unit of the synagogue was ten men who gathered to pray. ...a few inscriptions have been located from ancient synagogues in the NT era and they are distinctive in that they are in Greek uncials written in the Hellenistic style (i.e. from a later period than the life of Jesus). ...The gospel narratives mention a number of small towns in Galilee and the synagogues where Jesus taught. An additional group in this area has been excavated. They are small buildings with porches and columns, often...with stone seats and outer porticos. They must have served as law courts, schools, libraries and market places as well as for the Sabbath services."] The sole temple, or dedicated building of worship, was the one found in Jerusalem and destroyed in 70 AD.

It was the spirit of Constantine, not the Holy Spirit, that encouraged holy temple buildings.

The word *synagogue* means a meeting or assembly, and it is the meeting that makes it a synagogue, not the building or place. *Synagogy* is a Greek word for interactive discussion. When we think of Jewish meetings, we would benefit from thinking of them as a verb rather than a noun. In Matthew 9:35, where we read that Jesus went about all the cities and villages teaching in their synagogues and preaching about the kingdom, it means that He taught wherever they met in groups and interacted concerning the kingdom reality. His sheep were primarily out in the pasture, so to speak, and not in the sheepfold. He found them in the marketplaces of life, not in the worship centers of Israel.

In an important text in John 10:1-18, it is Jesus the Good Shepherd who does not keep the sheep locked up in the sheepfold.

He leads them out to find pasture! The spirit of Rome led to a fortress mentality regarding the church. By this I mean that the conversion of Constantine and the building of State funded churches placed emphasis on the location of the service rather than the service of the members to the world and to each other. The Spirit of Christ leads Christians out into the world to be salt and light.

Jesus and the Thief

Jesus then taught about the thief. I have heard many sermons that make the thief out to be the devil. "The devil," the preachers say, "has come to steal, kill, and destroy." Nothing could be further from the truth! It wasn't the devil that Jesus was referring to as the thief—it was the hireling shepherd. He was referring to the paid religious leadership of that day. The devil may come in sheep's clothing, but the thief in the warning of Jesus came in the robes of the priest. Could this also be true of some pastors in our day?

In this same text, Jesus said He had sheep not of the fold of Israel. We read this in John 10:16: "And other sheep I have that are not of this fold; them also I must bring, and they will hear My voice, and there will be one flock and one shepherd." We find that Jesus was quoting from Isaiah 42:1-9, where we read, "I will put My Spirit upon Him and He will bring forth justice to the Gentiles.... He will establish justice in all the Earth.... He will be a light to the Gentiles." This is the gospel of Jesus, the Savior of the *whole* world.

Jesus, Born to Die

Death and humility were such a part of the life of the King of heaven that even His birth foretold of His death mission. We all know Jesus was born in Bethlehem, but where in the city was the birth? According to the Gospel of Luke, in 2:7 we read as follows, "And she brought forth her first born Son, and wrapped Him in swaddling clothes, and laid Him in a manger, because there was no room in the inn." There is much significance in all the details of Jesus' birth.

I believe that our traditions have all but destroyed the real message in this unusual birth. At Christmas most homes, including mine, display a Nativity scene with a manger designed much like the ones European and early American farmers used for holding hay. We even have a cow in the manger scene. This is hardly what you would have seen if you had been with the first visitors, the shepherds. If you travel to Bethlehem today and find the Church of the Nativity, it is built over a cave. It is very probable that the innkeeper had a herd of sheep that were in the fields with the shepherd at the time of Christ's birth. The sheepfold would have been empty. What did it look like?

History tells us that the caves of Israel were often used as shelters for men and animals during the lifetime of the owner. Usually there was a part of the cave that would have been kept clean and reserved as the burial place for the owner upon his death. This is an important detail. It is very probable that the innkeeper offered this storage part of the cave as shelter for Mary and Joseph.

Outside the cave would have been a stone fence arranged to keep the animals from wandering during bad weather when they were kept in the sheepfold. Probably the outer cave held the stored grain and feed for the sheep. It would not have been unusual for guests of the inn in this little town to overflow into this sheltered area. Many travelers in that day stayed outside or found shelter like this cave.

What is the significance of the manger and swaddling clothes?

In the same Luke text, in 2:12 we read about the sign for the shepherds, "And this will be a sign unto you, you shall find the baby wrapped in swaddling clothes, lying in a manger." So, what is so unusual about these two items? All babies were wrapped in swaddling clothes (strips of cloth that were wrapped tightly around the baby), and any baby born in this cave might be placed in a manger. What else would you have used as a baby bed? But why are these signs important?

The swaddling clothes sign is important because this description is also used for the wrap used in preparing a dead body for burial. Remember when Lazarus was raised from the dead? He came forth wrapped in a swaddling cloth. It is probable that the owner of the inn had already placed the swaddling cloth in the cave in preparation for his future death and burial. It is also probable that Mary and Joseph were not prepared for the birth and upon finding the swaddling cloth (burial shroud), as was the custom in that day, wrapped the newborn Jesus, not realizing it was a shroud cloth of death. What a picture! Jesus was born to die for His sheep that He might lead them into their own deaths and then out to live in the lush, green pastures. I believe that only by experiencing a death of our egotistical selves can we become humble enough to enter the spiritual kingdom of heaven and rule there with Jesus.

As to the manger, this is an unfortunate word. The wooden mangers we are familiar with were not used in ancient Israel. The little feeding box was probably a stone trough. A better word would have been feeding trough for sheep. Guess what this means? Jesus, Himself, would later become the food for His sheep. Remember what we learned in chapter one? We must eat His flesh and drink His blood to become one with Him. Jesus was born not only to die but also to give His very life as spiritual food for His sheep. Does this Christmas scene now mean more as a true sign for you?

Jesus said He is the truth and that His flesh and His blood are true bread and true wine. Unless we feast on Him, co-mingle ourselves in union with Him, we cannot enter His kingdom or live from His kingdom resources. This is why Jesus said in John 4:24, "God is Spirit, and those who worship Him must worship Him in spirit and in truth."

Worship in spirit and in truth is not singing, praying, raising hands, and hearing sermons. These may or may not become true worship. True worship is only found in a change of lifestyle, when a follower of Jesus gives up his or her life and appropriates Jesus' life instead. True worship occurs when we end our lifetime ego trip and become humble servants of God and of mankind. I believe that Mother Teresa was such a servant and lived empowered by heavenly kingdom love. Don't you agree?

Now, in this light, read what John said in John 4:19-24—"The woman said to Him, 'Sir, I perceive that You are a prophet. Our fathers worshiped on this mountain, and you Jews say that in Jerusalem is the place where one ought to worship.' Jesus said to her, 'Woman, believe Me, the hour is coming when you will neither on this mountain, nor in Jerusalem, worship the Father. You worship what you do not know; we know what we worship, for salvation is of the Jews. But the hour is coming, and now is, when the true worshipers will worship the Father in spirit and truth; for the Father is seeking such to worship Him. God is Spirit, and those who worship Him must worship in spirit and truth.'"

Could it be that the will of God expressed in the life of Jesus would direct us away from pride, away from selfish ego, away from holy buildings, away from sacrifices for sin, away from controlling religious leaders and toward our own personal cross? Are we willing to end our emphasis on all of these and accept roles as servant shepherds in the kingdom of heaven?

Interactive Discussion Questions

1. According to Jesus in the John 4 text, does the place where we worship really matter? What might this mean to us today?
2. Is it possible that "we worship what we do not know"?
3. What does worship in spirit and in truth mean to you?
4. Is our worship only seeking God, or is it more important that the Father seeks us?
5. Of what importance is performing spiritual worship and the fact that God is spirit?
6. If Jesus was born to die, what might true spiritual worship mean in our lives?
7. Do you feel like you are living in the heavenly kingdom right now? Why or why not?
8. How does the life of Mother Teresa represent a life that was lived in the present kingdom?
9. Why might today's Christians stress correctness of doctrine and miss loving acts to the poor?
10. What most surprised you about the writer's picture of the birth of Jesus in Bethlehem?
11. If we have been born again, born of the Spirit, are we not "born in the manger as food for our fellow sheep," and are we not also to be "wrapped in the shroud cloth of death"? What should this mean in our lives?
12. Why do you think it is that Jesus made humility an entrance requirement for the kingdom of heaven, and how do you see that Jesus used the role of servant shepherd to illustrate humility? Are you living this way?

Chapter 6
Toppling The Ten Commandments
Jesus and the Law

"The Alabama Supreme Court has ruled that Judge Roy Moore of Gadsden, Alabama, may continue to open court sessions with prayer, and that he may continue to keep a plaque of the Ten Commandments on the wall of the Etowah County courtroom. The decision was 4–0, with five justices recuing themselves from the case." (January 24, 1998—Montgomery, Alabama (United Press International release)

Christians Today and the Law
The Christian's relationship to the Law is as fresh as recent news, such as the United Press International release above. Nothing will stir up the fervor of the Christian community more than an attack against the right of individuals to public expression of prayer and to honoring the Ten Commandments.

What should our attitude be toward the Ten Commandments in the age of grace? Are the Ten Commandments a perfect expression of the will of God for all times and all peoples? Do we as a society need to honor and obey these commandments, and if Jesus were living today, what would He do?

Mark Twain on the Ten Commandments
American humorist Mark Twain wrote on this subject in the early 1900s. He was not interested in the religious significance of the Law but was interested in how the Law related to the nature of man. I include a section of his essay, ("The Ten Commandments" from *Fables of Man*, found in the Mark Twain Papers Series of the University of California Press.)

"The Ten Commandments were made for man alone. We should think it strange if they had been made for all the animals.

99

We should say "Thou shalt not kill" is too general, too sweeping. It includes the field mouse and the butterfly. They can't kill. And it includes the tiger, which can't help it.

It is a case of Temperament and Circumstance again. You can arrange no circumstances that can move the field mouse and the butterfly to kill; their temperaments will ill keep them unaffected by temptations to kill, they can avoid that crime without an effort. But it isn't so with the tiger. Throw a lamb in his way when he is hungry, and his temperament will compel him to kill it.

Butterflies and field mice are common among men; they can't kill, their temperaments make it impossible. There are tigers among men, also. Their temperaments move them to violence, and when circumstance furnishes the opportunity and the powerful motive, they kill. They can't help it.

No penal law can deal out justice; it must deal out injustice in every instance. Penal laws have a high value, in that they protect—in a considerable measure—the multitude of the gentle-natured from the violent minority.

For a penal law is a circumstance. It is a warning which intrudes and stays a would-be murderer's hand—sometimes. Not always, but in many and many a case. It can't stop the real man-tiger; nothing can do that.

But the phrase is wrong, anyway. The word is the wrong word. Criminal courts do not dispense "justice"—they can't; they only dispense protections to the community. It is all they can do."

Interesting comments, I think, even if we do not totally agree with Mark Twain. He knew that the temperament had to be changed in order to change the ultimate behavior. The idea of a killer-mouse or grass-eating tiger both seem equally ridiculous. But a human is neither a mouse nor a tiger, although some may act like their animal cousins in these ways. How do we change mankind from killer temperament to kindness? That is the question.

100

How Is Human Temperament and Action Changed?

While laws and penalties may inhibit the killer temperament in humans, no law will stop killing under every circumstance. With enough inflammation of the emotions, probably almost any person could be moved to kill. Still, some gentle souls would never kill under any circumstance. But it is not the law "Thou shall not kill" that makes the difference, is it? The Law simply set forth a standard and then set penalties for those who broke it. The Law cannot change the heart of mankind. It may inhibit the worst passions, but it cannot remove them. What, then, did Jesus have to say about the Law?

Fulfillment Versus Obedience

Jesus said in Matthew 5:17, "Do not think that I came to destroy the Law or the Prophets. I did not come to destroy but to fulfill." What did He mean? Why not simply say, "to destroy the Law" and not mention the Prophets? I can understand why Jesus said He would fulfill the Prophets, to fulfill all prophecy, but how does one fulfill the Law? Did Jesus always obey the Ten Commandments?

As always, the context is very important. Jesus spoke the following words just before saying He would not destroy the Law but would fulfill it: "Let your light so shine before men, that they may see your good works and glorify your Father in heaven." So we find that Jesus wanted to be seen not as a rebel who taught people to disobey the Law and display evil works but as one who taught people to exceed the obedience required by the Law, thereby fulfilling, or expressing, the full significance of the Law. Because this was His intent, He also said in verse 20, "For I say to you, that unless your righteousness exceed the righteousness of the scribes and Pharisees, you will by no means enter the kingdom of heaven."

These sayings of Jesus seem to teach that He came to live in complete agreement with the Law, the Ten Commandments, and to accept the Jewish religion, while also presenting and demanding a new way of life that was in sharp contrast to the Jewish ways. The Jesus who befriended and accepted notorious sinners would

101

certainly be accused of being a person who dishonored the Law as expressed in the Ten Commandments. If He had placed ultimate honor on the commandment "Thou shall not commit adultery" and the penalty set by the Old Testament law, He would have had to pick up a stone and join in the stoning of the woman taken in adultery.

Christians Today Tend to Honor the Ten Commandments but Deny Their Penalty

Somehow, we want to accept the Law of God in the Ten Commandments and then deny the required penalty of that law. But we cannot in fairness pick and choose which part to honor and which part to destroy. The same Law and Prophets of the Old Testament that pronounced in the seventh commandment "Thou shall not commit adultery" also set the penalty for disobedience as death, claiming that God spoke to Moses in Leviticus 20:10 saying, "The man who commits adultery with another man's wife, he who commits adultery with his neighbor's wife, the adulterer and the adulteress, shall surely be put to death."

It is sentimental nonsense to honor the laws in the Ten Commandments and then to dishonor the Prophets by refusing to administer the penalties required for breaking those laws.

Should Our Courts Display Both the Laws and the Punishments?

Why did Judge Roy Moore insist on displaying the Ten Commandments without also displaying the Ten Punishments? I think we know the answer. But we cannot have it both ways—we cannot honor part of the Law and the Prophets and then dishonor another part simply because we find it too barbaric. Yet this is what we all do, Jew and Christian alike.

This makes the response of Jesus even more brilliant when the religious leaders asked Him, "Now Moses, in the law, commanded us that such should be stoned. But what do You say?" Jesus did not say to break the penalty part of the Law; He simply pointed out that the Law was such a high standard that it condemned every man, so *either stone no one or stone everybody!* This event was not

102

unique in the life of Christ. He also stood against the Law and the Prophets. Jesus purposely broke many of the commandments and taught others to break them as well. Surprised? You won't be if you know your gospel stories well.

Jesus the Notorious Law Breaker

Let me ask if you keep the Ten Commandments as a Christian? What day did you attend worship services—on Saturday, the Sabbath, or on Sunday? You, who claim with Judge Roy Moore that the Ten Commandments are the basis for all law for all time, probably without even thinking, break the fourth commandment every week. But, you protest, we have substituted the Sunday worship for the Sabbath worship.

Jesus was willing to break the Sabbath laws because He taught, "The Sabbath was made for man, and not man for the Sabbath." By extension, man was not made for the Law, but the Law was made for man. For this reason Jesus taught that obedience of the letter of the law was not as important as obedience of the royal law, the law of love.

We Pick the Laws We Will Obey and Those We Will Conveniently Change and Avoid!

Now, take a minute to think about this! Do you realize that by taking this position you are actually saying that the Laws of the Ten Commandments are subject to modification based on private interpretation? This could open the proverbial can of worms. Why not change the sixth commandment—"Thou shalt not kill"—to something a little more acceptable, such as "Thou shalt not kill unless sufficiently provoked; or the seventh to "Thou shalt have sex only with someone you really love"; or the ninth to "Thou shalt tell white lies whenever they serve your purpose."

Perhaps you think this is ludicrous, but the fact is, many people, and even most Christians, live like this today. We unthinkingly say we want to fulfill the Law, but do we really— especially if we all deserve to be stoned? If you want to return to the good old days under the Law, remember the following penalties for the infractions of the Ten Commandments (my facetious comments are added):

Our Ten Commandments in Practice

Exodus 22:20—"He who sacrifices to any god, except to the LORD only, he shall be utterly destroyed." Well, there goes most of us because we sacrifice almost everything to the gods of materialism and success!

Deuteronomy 13:10—"And you shall stone him with stones until he dies, because he sought to entice you away from the LORD your God." Again, we had better stone all NFL football players because they have taken our commitment to the Lord on Sunday and turned it into the worship of sports.

Leviticus 24:16—"And whoever blasphemes the name of the LORD shall surely be put to death. All the congregation shall certainly stone him." There goes much of our television and movie entertainment!

Exodus 31:15—"Whoever does any work on the Sabbath day (Saturday) shall surely be put to death." I like this one! Don't you dare tempt me to mow the lawn on Saturday!

Exodus 21:15—"He that strikes his father or his mother shall surely be put to death." Old man, if you ever lay a hand on me again, I will knock you from today into next year!

Exodus 21:17—"He who curses his father or mother shall surely be put to death." But you don't know what my father did to me! If you did you would join me in exposing him to the whole world.

Exodus 21:22-25—"If men fight and hurt a woman with child…if any lasting harm follows, then you shall give life for life, eye for eye, tooth for tooth, hand for hand, foot for foot, burn for burn, wound for wound, stripe for stripe." I guess we have every reason to bomb, kill, cripple, and maim all the people in any Muslim country because, after all, they are only being repaid for 9/11!

Leviticus 20:10—"The man who commits adultery with another man's wife, and he who commits adultery with his neighbor's wife, the adulterer and the adulteress shall surely be put to death." I suppose we would have no problem with the population explosion if every person who was unfaithful in marriage were put to death. Oh, by the way, according to Jesus just the desire to commit adultery is breaking the law. Who might be left alive now?

Exodus 22:2—"If the thief is found breaking in, and he is struck so that he dies, there shall be no guilt for his bloodshed." Great! Let's arm the neighborhoods and kill anyone who dares enter our homes without permission.

Deuteronomy 19:18-19—"If the witness is a false witness, then you shall do to him as he thought to do to his brother, so you shall put away the evil person from among you." What if all gossipers were treated as if their gossip was intended to hurt others? Shut my mouth, Lord!

Exodus 20:17—"You shall not covet." Finally, a law I could break and not get stoned! There was no direct penalty for coveting, because coveting is an attitude, not an action. Nevertheless, this law is the foundation for all the others. To covet means to strongly desire what is not my own. If I covet, it can lead to: love of things over God; idolatry; swearing in God's name to get my way; working every day for stuff; secretly hoping my daddy dies soon so I can spend his money; murder of anyone who keeps me from getting what I believe should be mine; liking my neighbor's wife more than my own; taking what I want from the office because it will not be missed; lying about others so as to make myself look good. Oh well, as Jesus taught, even the intent of my heart is open to God's judgment, so I am guilty even if the penalty is not stoning.

Perhaps you have never noted this verse in Malachi 2:2-3: "If ye will not hear and if ye will not lay it to heart, to give glory to my name, saith the Lord of hosts, I will even curse you,...I will corrupt your seed and spread dung upon your faces" (KJV). The God of the Old Testament is apparently very serious about a heart change, wouldn't you agree? Are we actually listening today?

So, who gets away without being stoned? Not me! Are you getting the point? The Law only makes us obviously guilty of falling short of God's high intention for mankind. Let's stop kidding ourselves. If we were to return to the days of Jewish law, we would all revolt. So let's stop giving the Law such a prominent place in our world if we do not intend to fulfill it by loving others as Jesus commanded.

Jesus' Demands Are Above the Law

What if we understood that Jesus' fulfillment of the Law was something so radical that the Law became much, much less important to us than His life of love? I believe it is very evident to anyone who looks at the Old Testament Law and punishments that Jesus had to make a change for the benefit of all humanity. *The focus had to be moved from law to love.* Nothing else would have released society to progress beyond the barbaric systems of law and punishment.

Why do so many Christians remain stuck on an emphasis of right living according to the Law when Jesus taught that love fulfills the Law? The righteous indignation of modern Christians, when they say they are not under the Law, reveals they cannot accept such freedom. The normal response to an emphasis on love alone is to say, this makes us sentimental do-gooders rather than real moral Christians. This response indicates a misunderstanding of the power of grace and love. The church of today is into sin management and not into being loving or spiritual.

Why Not Place the Demand of Jesus in the Court House?

Jesus' controlling principle was expressed in Matthew 5:43-45. You will see He shows that the spirit of the kingdom of heaven demands more than the Ten Commandments and that His concept of God is dramatically different from the way the Old Testament people saw God. "You have heard that it was said, 'You shall love your neighbor but hate your enemy.' But I say to you, love your enemies, bless those who curse you, do good to those who hate you, and pray for those who spitefully use you and persecute you, that you may be sons of your Father in heaven; for He makes His sun rise on the evil and the good, and sends rain on the just and the unjust."

106

Jesus Came Primarily to Correct a Wrong Concept of God!

Which picture of God do you prefer, the spiteful God who will condemn you and turn His back on you if you fail to glorify Him or the God and Father presented by Jesus who loves His enemies and is kind to everyone? Jesus is too radical for most of us today. Unfortunately, we think we must preserve the God of wrath presented in the Old Testament lest we be too soft on sin. Jesus reserved the wrath of God for only those few religious leaders who twisted the loving God into a vengeful God for their own manipulative purposes. (See Matthew 12:34 and 23:33 that clearly shows the negative attitude of Jesus toward the Pharisees generally.)

Jesus Seldom Warned Sinners to Stop Sinning

It is important to point out that Jesus never warned a sinner about the coming wrath of God. He did, however, warn some people. Following is the only example of a warning of the coming wrath of God by Jesus, and it is found in Luke 21:20-24:

"But when you see Jerusalem surrounded by armies, then know that its desolation is near. Then let those in Judea flee to the mountains, let those who are in the midst of her depart, and let not those who are in the country enter her. For these are the days of vengeance, that all things which are written may be fulfilled. But woe to those who are pregnant and those who are nursing babies in those days. For there will be great distress in the land and wrath upon this people. And they will fall by the edge of the sword and be led away captive into all nations. And Jerusalem will be trampled by Gentiles until the times of the Gentiles are fulfilled."

Jesus was describing the coming destruction of the temple in Jerusalem by Rome, and it occurred in A.D. 70. The wrath of God that was predicted for those who rejected the Messiah was completed at that time.

John the Baptist had foreknown this wrath, and he spoke of it in Luke 3:7-8: "Then he said to the multitudes that came out to be

107

baptized by him, 'Brood of vipers! Who warned you to flee from the wrath to come? Therefore bear fruits worthy of repentance, and do not begin to say to yourselves, "We have Abraham as our father." For I say to you that God is able to raise up children to Abraham from these stones.'" And He did. God made His special relationship with Abraham available to Gentiles all over the world, who, like the stones, were incapable of becoming God's special children without a miracle.

Jesus did not condemn sinners. He condemned the religious leaders, the Pharisees, Sadducees, and scribes. Contrast John 3:17 and Matthew 23:33 to see the difference. "For God did not send His Son into the world to condemn the world, but that the world through Him might be saved." Compare this to, "Serpents, brood of vipers, how can you escape the condemnation of Hell?" You can see the difference.

You may wonder, what about the rich? They, too, were not people's favorites in that era. Jesus warned that riches may prevent men from entering the kingdom, but He sorrowed over their condition and said that with God all things are possible. He lovingly warned them but never condemned them. He warned about a general wrath to come on the land of Israel, but He did not warn everyday sinners about eternal wrath, their exclusion from the kingdom of heaven. In fact, this is what He said: "Assuredly, I say to you that tax collectors and harlots enter the kingdom of God before you" (Matthew 21:31b).

Note what He did not say. He did not say the tax collectors, who were really sophisticated thieves, and the harlots, who regularly broke the commandments against adultery, stopped their wicked practices. He simply said that they entered the kingdom. What precipitated this? Their salvation was based simply on their humble admission of their need, as opposed to the religious rulers' denial of their need. Some obviously changed their behavior, but not all did, or the Scriptures would have made this distinction. In fact, Paul said clearly in Romans 4:5, quoting David, "But to him who does not work but believes on Him who justifies the ungodly, his faith is accounted for righteousness." Ungodly people who have as yet not changed are clearly justified by faith in a God who "Does not count their sins against them."

Which do you really prefer, the God Jesus presented as the God of grace and love or the God of wrath and laws that the ancient Jews believed ruled over humanity? Lest you think this is a false choice and there is no difference, let me remind you that Jesus' teachings contrasted these two views of God. The covenant of law and the covenant of grace are that different in their views of God. This is why we have an Old and New Testament.

I believe that God never really changed, only the human perception of Him was altered. Jesus brought the major change to human understanding with His depiction of God as a loving Father as in Matthew 7:7-12, "Ask, and it will be given to you; seek, and you will find; knock, and it will be opened to you. For everyone who asks receives, and he who seeks finds, and to him who knocks it will be opened. Or what man is there among you who, if his son asks for bread, will give him a stone? Or if he asks for a fish, will he give him a serpent? If you then, being evil, know how to give good gifts to your children, how much more will your Father who is in heaven give good things to those who ask Him!" (emphasis mine)

Interactive Discussion Questions

1. Why do you think modern Christians in America are so determined to honor the Ten Commandments but fail to present the punishments required by those laws?
2. What do you receive from the teaching of Mark Twain regarding the laws and the issue of temperament?
3. Is it unlawful and morally wrong for a tiger to kill to eat?
4. Do you believe that knowledge of the law and threatened punishment can eliminate crime?
5. What do you feel about the statement that modern Christians are into sin management more than into spirituality and becoming loving?
6. How effective is the sin management in our society?
7. Why might grace and love be more powerful than law?
8. If the punishments are no longer believed to be just and are seen as barbaric, why are we not able to see that the laws themselves may change in different cultures and times?
9. If the Law says, "You shall not covet your neighbor's wife," is it all right for a wife to covet her neighbor's husband? Based on the fact that in that time women were the property of their husbands, should the Law reflect gender equality today? Why or why not?
10. What is the difference between Jesus' fulfilling the Law and Jesus' obeying the Law?
11. How is the Law fulfilled, according to Jesus?
12. Are you uncomfortable with de-emphasizing the Law and placing more emphasis on grace and love? Why or why not?
13. Of law and grace, which is based on fear, and which is based on love?

Chapter 7
Jesus – Rebel With a Cause
Jesus and disobedience

Have you ever been between the proverbial rock and a hard place? At some point in life most of us are forced to decide between two options: the greater good or the lesser evil. Life is often like that.

Extreme cases come to mind, such as the African mother living through a drought with two babies to care for. The mother might willingly forgo her own need for food to feed the babies, but what happens when there is only enough food for one child? If the mother gives both babies only a small amount, probably both will die soon. If the mother feeds one, keeps nothing for herself, and then does not feed the other child, at least one might survive until help comes. What would you do?

As Christians, we react against the idea of situational ethics, but how are we to make the right decisions in life when faced with conflicting situations like these? The law, or the restraints of cultural rights and wrongs, may not always be enough to override our hearts. We know we make some decisions simply because we find more emotional reasons for that decision. We may not want to get into such choices, but sometimes life seems to require this of us. As a counselor, I have often been presented with these conundrums. It would sometimes be easier to just be legalistic or moralistic about the judgments and let the counseling client "simmer in his own stew."

Ben and Being Right
For example, think about this story. Ben was a good man, a believer, the father of two boys and the husband of a pretty wife. Ben had always been faithful to his family. Then life took a difficult turn. He was offered a job that was great for his career, and the increase in income was sufficient to make the family very comfortable.

Enter Kathy! Kathy, Ben told me, was the new secretary in his marketing department. She was a pretty brunette with beautiful but

111

sad eyes. While they did not work together directly, he saw her every day. One day upon his arrival at work he found Kathy crying at her desk. Since no one else was around he felt it was his responsibility to find out why she was crying. Ben, you see, was a good man.

Good Men Sometimes Take Great Risks

As Ben told the story to me in a session, he recounted how his heart went out to her when he heard her husband had left her with many bills, three children and only her meager secretarial salary. She did not even know how to contact him. Now the creditors were dogging her, and the mortgage company was about to foreclose on their home. This, she said, was not Ben's problem, but she needed to talk to someone.

The plot thickens! Ben had recently invested some of his increased income in the stock market with a vow to God that he would use some of the profits for ministry. Since Ben had just sold some of the stock for a considerable profit and had some extra money in his checking account, he considered telling Betty about Kathy and her needs. However, he knew from past experience that Betty was very insecure and any thought of his even talking to Kathy, let alone helping her, would lead to a big argument. Betty was not interested in his investments and had told Ben to handle the investment account on his own and never to discuss it with her.

For these reasons Ben decided to help Kathy without telling Betty. Over Kathy's objections, Ben wrote her a check. Ben felt good.

Kathy, thankful for his help but confused over which bills to pay and how to handle the creditors, asked for Ben's help. Ben agreed to drop by her home, meet her three children, and take some time to look at her finances. Having completed this task, as he left, Kathy gave him a grateful hug and a quick kiss. Ben felt uncomfortable but reasoned it was just an expression of friendship and thankfulness. Ben told me he had no romantic or sexual interest in Kathy, only a sense of a special bond of friendship. Apparently Kathy felt the same way.

Weeks later Ben and Betty went to a T-ball game on a Saturday with their boys, and guess who was on the opposing team? Sam, one of Kathy's boys. He came running up to Ben after the game and thanked him for helping his mom—right in front of a shocked Betty. Then Kathy gave Ben a hug and gathered her children into her car, leaving Ben and Betty in the circumstance that brought Ben to my office. Being sure that Ben was having an affair, Betty had moved out to her mother's apartment, leaving Ben with the boys and a broken, confused heart.

Ben was so upset over Betty's leaving him that he couldn't eat, and he was missing work because he had to take care of the boys. His life went from the high of being a rescuer to the low of being seen as a cheating husband. Even his pastor had turned against him. How, he asked me, could God allow this to happen when his heart motive was only good?

At this point, the easy thing would have been to instruct Ben in what he should have done, to give him the rules of a proper marriage. But what about that Scripture verse in James that spoke to Ben, "Pure and undefiled religion before God and the Father is this: to visit orphans and widows in their trouble, and to keep oneself unspotted from the world" (James 1:27).

Ben had done almost exactly that. He had helped a woman whose situation was similar to that of a widow and had helped some almost orphaned children. And he had kept himself unspotted—he had not done this good deed expecting any favors, especially nothing romantic or sexual. However, because Betty's father had had an affair and left her mom and Betty when she was young she distrusted men and had jumped to her own conclusions where Ben and Kathy were concerned.

Ben loved Betty and knew her reaction was based on her past, but he had not thought out the impact his secrecy and actions would have on her. Betty had made her share of bad decisions, too. She let her fears fire her imagination and her anger at men to unjustly control her tongue, making a difficult situation much worse.

I will leave the story there because my intent is not to explain my counseling approach, good or bad. Neither is it my intent to have you choose sides with either Ben or Betty, but I want us to think about love. What was the loving thing to do in this situation? Don't moralize or feel sorry for Ben or Betty based on your own prejudices or experiences. Think about how our actions of loving people will sometimes place us at risk. Think about why we Christians usually think rules will protect us from the inherent risk of being loving.

Is Motive More Important Than Method?

The Bible does not always present easy answers either, and life and love are sometimes messy. If we modern Christians had our way, based on the biblical passage in James, we probably would have instructed Ben to only get involved with Kathy and her kids in tandem with his wife Betty, right? Or perhaps Ben should have asked a compassion-based ministry committee in his church to minister to her.

Perhaps Betty should have confirmed every rumor she heard with two or more witnesses before reacting. Or perhaps God will use this pain in Betty's life to send her for counseling to get free from past hurts, and perhaps she will be confronted with the need to forgive and not become bitter.

Maybe all the pain in Ben's life is for a purpose, too. Perhaps he is learning to love, and for this he is to be encouraged. Perhaps Ben needs friendship and encouragement more than moralizing and meaningless "should haves." Before we judge Ben or Betty too harshly, think about the following biblical stories and how they might relate to their situation.

The Test of Abraham

Abraham, the father of the faith, was presented with a dilemma when God asked him to sacrifice his son Isaac. God was faithful, and after many, many years brought the son of promise, Isaac, into the marriage of Sarah and Abraham. This was the child they had always dreamed about. This was the child through whom God had promised Abraham that his children would become many, like the sand of the seashore. Through Isaac, all the world would be blessed. God had promised this. And now God made a demand of love—a seemingly not very loving demand toward Abraham and certainly not very loving toward Isaac.

We read about this love test in Genesis 22:1-2, "Now it came to pass that after these things God tested Abraham, and said to him, 'Abraham!' and he said, 'Here I am.' Then He said, 'Take now your son, your only son Isaac, whom you love, and go to the land of Moriah, and offer him there as a burnt offering on one of the mountains of which I shall tell you.'"

Must Every Test of Love Be Openly Discussed and Shared?

Do you suppose that Abraham told his wife, Sarah, what he was about to do? Do you suppose that Sarah would have intervened and stopped this potential killing of her son? Probably this love test between Abraham's love of God and his love for Isaac was a personal thing, and I doubt that Sarah even knew about it.

The sacrifice of children to an idol or a god was somewhat common in that land at that time. Later, God will tell the children of Abraham that he finds the sacrifice of children an abomination. Nevertheless, the test of love, the test of priorities, was placed before Abraham, and he did not fail. We know this because we know the rest of the story. Abraham trusted God and loved Him more than his special son of promise. In essence, Abraham loved the Promiser more than the promise, the Giver more than the gift. This test being fulfilled by Abraham's actions, God intervenes and provides an animal, a ram, for the sacrifice, and both Abraham and Isaac are spared.

The Testing of Jesus

In the Gospels we see that Jesus faced the test of love's priorities to the point of disobedience of one of the Ten Commandments. Here is the commandment—"Honor your father and your mother as the Lord God has commanded you" (Deuteronomy 5:16). The test Jesus placed on His disciples in Luke 14:26, "If anyone comes to Me and does not hate his father and mother, wife and children, brothers and sisters, yea and his own life also, he cannot be My disciple." Matthew 8:21-22—"a

115

disciple said to Him, Lord, first let me go bury my father and Jesus said to him, ' Follow Me, and let the dead bury their own dead." Obviously, to leave a dead father without proper burial was a great dishonor, but Jesus did not simply challenge His disciples to break the love-of-parent commandment. He Himself did it.

Jesus illustrated the prioritization of love by placing the demands of the kingdom of heaven and the demands of His heavenly Father above the rights of His own mother, brothers, and sisters. In Matthew 12:47-50 we read the story, "Then one of them said to Him, 'Look, your mother and your brothers are standing outside, seeking to speak with You.' But He answered and said to the one who told Him, 'Who is My mother and who are My brothers?' And He stretched out His hand toward the disciples and said, 'Here are My mother and My brothers. For whoever does the will of My Father in heaven is My brother and sister and My mother.'"

It is apparent from this text that Jesus' mother and brothers came seeking Him, and He snubbed them in favor of His followers. But what else might Jesus be teaching? I believe that the love required in the kingdom of heaven overrules the love required on earth, and the love required by the law. Therefore, we can say that when Jesus broke one of the Ten Commandments, He replaced it with the higher law, the law of love in the kingdom of heaven. When Jesus said He would not destroy the Law but fulfill it, this did not mean that He would not break the Law. He broke the Law, but always replaced it with the higher law of love. In this way He fulfilled, or completed, the intent of the Law. Think about how this might apply to Ben?

David's Sin

Then there is the case of David, the anointed and promised king of Israel, the man after God's own heart. He had no higher reason for breaking a moral law of God when he took Bathsheba as his lover, got her pregnant, had her husband killed, and then took her as his own wife. In this case David lived in justifiable guilt until confronted by the prophet. He then said a troubling thing when he repented, "Against Thee, God, and Thee alone have I sinned."

Well hardly! I guess if I were Bathsheba's husband, Uriah, I could have claimed that the sin was against me. Besides, when Nathan the prophet accused David, it was with a story of a rich man stealing a poor man's only sheep. So David had sinned against Uriah and knew it.

What could his prayer to God (saying that his sin was against God alone) mean? I believe that in their society if David, as king, had asked Uriah for his wife, the loyal Uriah would have given her to David. That was the way many kings developed their harems. I believe that David had the right to order how his men were to fight in battle, but he had no excuse for breaking the higher law. The higher law is to love God supremely, then love your neighbor, as Jesus later taught. David's actions show us that he had elevated himself above his neighbor, and even above God. He was not willing to wait for an answer from Uriah, and certainly not waiting for God's solution. He had not acted in love but in lust. He had covered his sin. He had acted unloving to all concerned, including God.

David and Bearing False Witness

This was not the only time he broke a commandment. David knew full well that lying was against God's Law. The Law said, "You shall not bear false witness." Nevertheless, we find David bearing false witness and not being condemned for it in a story in 1 Samuel 21:12. David was in enemy territory and in danger of losing his life. In verse 12 we read, "Now David took the words to heart and was very much afraid of Achish, the king of Gath. So he changed his behavior before them, feigned madness in their hands, scratched on the doors of the gate, and let his saliva fall down his beard. Then Achish said to his servants, 'Look, you see the man is insane. Why have you brought him to me.'" The result was they let David go.

Why was this action of David, when he broke the false witness law and was honored and not condemned for it, recorded in Scripture? I believe it was because it was the greater good, the preservation of life over the telling of complete truth.

117

Rahab and Disobedience

Who else in Scripture was honored for lying? We remember the story of Rahab the harlot in Jericho. She is famous and so well regarded by God's Word that she makes the list of the faithful in Hebrews chapter 11. What did she do that saved her life and made her a standard of faith? She lied. She hardly gave true witness. In fact, she gave great false witness.

Here is the story in Joshua 2:4-5. "The woman [Rahab] took the two men [Israelite spies] and hid them; and she said, 'Yes the men [spies] came to me, but I did not know where they were from [lie one]. And it happened as the gate was being shut, when it was dark, that the men went out [lie two]. Where the men went I do not know [lie three]; Pursue them quickly, for you may overtake them [lie four].'" [inserts mine]

For this breaking of the false-witness commandment, Rahab was physically saved from the destruction and death of Jericho, but the amazing thing is that it was Rahab's expression of faith that won her the coveted award of being in the special list of the faithful in the book of Hebrews. Why? There can be only one answer—the law of love in the spiritual kingdom of God was more important than the ninth commandment. Rahab proved she loved God and wanted what He wanted more than she loved her country, her city, or her reputation for truth. Are you beginning to get the principle? Love not only fulfills the commandments, sometimes it overrides them.

In Romans 2:28-29 the apostle Paul says this, "For he is not a Jew who is one outwardly, nor is that circumcision; which is outward in the flesh. But he is a Jew who is one inwardly, and circumcision is that of the heart, in the Spirit and not in the letter, whose praise is not from men, but from God." In light of our review in this chapter let me rephrase this.

Loving in Spirit Rather Than in Letter

Outward obedience of the law is not enough. If you have a changed heart, a heart of love, you obey not the letter of the law but the higher law, the law of love dictated by the Spirit to your spirit.

The people of Israel at the time of Christ labored under the Ten Commandments, a multitude of other laws, and detailed purity requirements to prove one was holy. There were 613 commandments, 365 prohibitions, and hundreds of lesser injunctions the people had to follow to be "good" Jews. Paul described the burden as being unbearable and too much for anyone to carry. He should have known, because he managed to follow the letter of the law perfectly as a Pharisee.

Can you see why Jesus said in Matthew 11:28, "Come unto Me, all you who labor and are heavy laden, and I will give you rest."? He really did! He exchanged the over seven hundred things Jews had to do for only two, "Love God, and love your neighbor as yourself." Simple and powerful, isn't it?

Jesus Disregarded the Laws of Purity

Jesus often broke the cultural purity laws of Israel by touching defiled people and by even touching the dead. This was strictly forbidden of a rabbi by the purity laws. Some examples come to mind including these: In Matthew 9:10-13 Jesus ate with known sinners. To do so made a religious person unclean in Israel. In Matthew 9:24-25 Jesus touched a dead girl and she came to life. Touching the dead made a religious person unclean. In Matthew 11:19 Jesus showed He could party hardy. He was accused of being a glutton and a winebibber, or heavy drinker. Such behavior made a religious person unclean.

In every case, the love Jesus had for people was more important to Him than any cultural taboo.

Cultural Taboos and Love over Law

David was known for breaking a cultural and religious taboo too. He profaned the temple by entering the holy place that was only available to priests and by taking the temple showbread from the table to eat and share with his men. This experience without God's punishment was quoted by Jesus to give Him the right to break the Sabbath law. In Matthew 12:1-8 Jesus and His disciples harvested grain and ate it on the Sabbath day. Jesus excused this

119

behavior based on David's experience. In Matthew 12:9-14 Jesus healed on the Sabbath, breaking the Sabbath law.

In every case, the law of love and needs of the people were more important to Jesus than strict obedience to the Law. Jesus wants us to learn this teaching in Mark 2:27—"The Sabbath was made for man, and not man for the Sabbath."

I want us to see that this is true of the whole law. It was made for man's benefit. Sabbath rest is important, but not for the rule itself. If loving a person in need would require one to break the Sabbath rules of rest, then Jesus would break that rule for the sake of love. If lying saved David's life, and Rahab's lies saved the spies from Israel, then the law is secondary to the law of love. What else can the life and teaching of Jesus mean?

The Clash of Jesus and the Law

In some cases Jesus overturned certain of the Ten Commandments. At the highest level, He declared Himself equal to God by using the sacred name of "I AM" for Himself (John 8:58). In so doing He refuted the "one God" teaching of the Jewish faith by making Himself equal to God.

Jesus lifted our lives above the Law by placing His Spirit of love in us that we might have His indwelling power to love even our enemies. As we avail ourselves of this love, we automatically live even better than the Law demands, and sometimes in spite of the Law's demands. Jesus said in Matthew 5:20, "For I say unto you, unless your righteousness exceeds the righteousness of the scribes and Pharisees, you will by no means enter the kingdom of heaven." We know that the righteousness demanded by the Pharisees was the legalistic following of rules, obeying the letter of the Law, as well as many additional letters. If this doesn't cut it in the kingdom, what could?

Difficult Decisions and Loving Lavishly

Love fulfills the Law, it exceeds the Law, and sometimes it replaces the Law. Difficult? Yes! But the requirements of the law of love are much more difficult than a simple statement of "thou shalt not." Jesus turned the many negative "thou shalt not" laws into two positives: Love God and love your neighbor as yourself. This is a summary of the position of Jesus and the Law (John 13:34): "A new commandment I give you, that you love one another."

Like it or not, Jesus was not legalistic and did not always obey the Law. His message of love over law caused the religious leaders to hate him. Religious people still hate this message. However, if Jesus had been the good religious Jewish boy, He would not have been crucified. Jesus was a radical without being rebellious against real spiritual truth. His law of love exceeds the requirements of the laws of mankind and even the Ten Commandments. Are we living in the power and the freedom of the Spirit of love?

Interactive Discussion Questions

1. Have you ever pictured Jesus as a law breaker?
2. How do you personally react to the story about Ben?
3. Which would Jesus judge as the greater sin, Ben's hidden act of love or Betty's judgment? Why?
4. Under the influence of the Spirit of God, Nathan confronted David. Was adultery the greatest of David's sins? How about the murder of Uriah? What was the central issue of condemnation against David?
5. How does the teaching of Jesus about the higher law, the law of love, apply to David's story?
6. It is not my desire to justify Ben's actions, but how might his actions have paralleled Jesus' rejection of His mother, Mary, and His brothers?
7. What is the practical significance of Ben's actions?
8. Where do the traditions of men and the taboos of culture come from? How might they parallel the teaching of Jesus about the law of love and how may they be in opposition to the teaching of Jesus?
9. Why do cultural taboos and traditions persist? What do we get out of them?
10. How might Ben have been more loving to everyone in his life?
11. What dominated Ben that he did not tell Betty about his decision --- fear or love?
12. If perfect love casts out fear, relate your experience with the Law, and answer this question: Does my obedience stem from fear or love?

Chapter 8
Jesus Lightens the Burden of the Law
Jesus' new commandment

Let me ask a question. What if the command of Jesus to love God and love your neighbor were practiced simply and spontaneously without our getting sidetracked with myriad rules and expectations? How would this lifestyle, the lifestyle of Jesus, change our lives and the lives of people around us? In essence, what would a person be like if he lived, not from this world's resources or according to the expectations of our culture, but to the tune of a different drummer, the heartbeat of the indwelling Spirit of love? How would life rooted in the kingdom of heaven grow and prosper and at the same time make a difference in the world?

Quality Versus Quantity

We reviewed Mother Teresa's life in an earlier chapter of this book. We remember that her magnificent servanthood given to the poorest of the poor resulted in her fame and ministry success. Her life was exceptional, not necessarily in quality of service—she ministered in simple ways, but certainly in quantity—she touched many thousands of lives. Most of us will never make such a large impact, but how about making a difference in at least a few people's lives? Wouldn't it be great if we were just a little like Mother Teresa?

It may surprise you, but Mother Teresa undoubtedly ministered to more poor people during her lifetime than Jesus did in His ministry on Earth. Certainly Billy Graham has shared the gospel message with greater multitudes than Jesus did. Almost any Bible-school president has trained more disciples than Jesus did. In the kingdom of heaven, numbers are not all that important.

Maximum Spiritual Power but Minimal Ministry

We possess the same Spirit that motivated Mother Teresa. We have the indwelling life of our Lord through the Holy Spirit – the source of invincible love. We are surrounded by similar needs, even if our culture is not as poor as that in Calcutta. So, why are we failing to manifest this new commandment of love Christ instructed us to share with others? Are we too distracted by bad things in our lives—family problems, difficult jobs, broken relationships, and so forth? Or perhaps we are overly busy with too many good things—Bible study, prayer meetings, choir practice, committees, etc. Are we, however, missing the best thing, the more excellent way?

Jesus is King of the kingdom of heaven and, as absolute ruler, He has the right and the responsibility to command His army. Yet we will note that Jesus reduced over seven hundred commandments to two, and He only gave two major marching instructions. In the church we know them as the Great Commandment and the Great Commission. Let's review these two commandments of Jesus by giving note to their order.

The Two Orders from Our Kingdom Commander

The Great Commandment to love was given before the Great Commission. I believe this is for a significant reason. In the Great Commission Jesus instructed His followers on how to share the gospel message with the whole world. But Jesus knew the world would not listen to this message if we did not precede the message with a methodology of love. Someone rightly said, "the world does not care how much you know (for example, about the teachings of Jesus) until they know how much you care."

Christianity has always spread fastest in those regions where missionary efforts were combined with building schools and hospitals, feeding the hungry, and other acts of loving assistance. I believe this was the expectation of Jesus—that we should love first and teach second. A great saint, I believe it was Saint Francis of Assisi, said, "Preach the gospel at all times, if necessary use words." How true this is.

The Jesus Style—Earthly Relief Rather Than Heavenly Promises

In an attempt to determine why the church so often fails to produce believers who manifest the love of Jesus, consider this. Is it possible that we have become more concerned for the conversion of people than for their earthly needs? You may respond to this question by saying their eternal destiny is much more important than their physical needs. Perhaps, but although this sounds good, I ask you to review the life of Jesus. He seldom shared what we might call the plan of salvation. He simply went around acting in a loving way. He was known as a good man and a healer, but no one ever called Him a great evangelist. Does this not say something about our misplaced priorities?

Mission Motive

Is it possible we might be sharing the gospel message about how to receive salvation out of a motive of being right and being in control more than out of a motive of love? Are we actually just trying to convert others to our way of thinking and believing? Can we really trust our heart motives? How can we say we love a person as a human being and not save their physical lives from starvation and bring healing to their broken hearts? Are we just to tell them about heaven? Many Christians with good intentions have corrupted the good news in this very way. The good news is that God loves people and motivates us to love them too. Any attempt to make them a success number by counting them as one of our converts, without also caring about their needs, is hardly good news.

Only when we first fulfill the Great Commandment to love can we powerfully expand the kingdom by the Great Commission. Jesus simplified the Law into His new commandment—love God and love your neighbor. We know the Great Commission tells us to "Go into all the world," but the Christian church has all too often attempted to fulfill the going without first giving. This is why the world sees us as self-righteous, as wanting to be right about our theories of God more than we want to be loving. When we get the Great Commandment down right, it will change our view of the Great Commission.

Jesus said, "'You shall love the Lord your God with all your heart, with all your soul, with all your mind.' This is the first and great commandment. The second is like it; 'You shall love your

125

neighbor as yourself.' On these two commandments hang all the Law and the Prophets" (Matthew 22:37-40).

I want to point out that Jesus taught that the entire Great Commission also hangs on love. I fear that we have made it into a marketing tool by offering eternal salvation to people who accept our statement of faith. There is less conversion-style evangelism in the Great Commission than we think, at least if we believe that the evangelical message is how to be returned to a right relationship with God and, thus, be saved from hell.

Without the Love Commandment We Are out of Commission!

Let's review Christ's second commandment, the Great Commission. We find it best stated in Matthew 28:19-20, "Go therefore and make disciples of all the nations, baptizing them in the name of the Father and the Son and the Holy Spirit, teaching them to observe all things I have commanded you; and lo, I am with you always, even to the end of the age. Amen." Christ's commission clearly directs us to do three things: disciple, baptize, and teach. These, by the way, take more work than just presenting the plan of salvation and simply asking for a decision. They take more time—discipleship took Jesus three intensive years with His twelve men. They take risk—in many countries baptism means a radical commitment that could result in death. This is hardly an easy decision approach to the gospel.

Another key point is found in the instructions regarding what we are to teach. What are the things that Jesus commanded us? Again we can go back to the simplicity of the gospel. In chapter 2 we discovered that the gospel of Jesus was all about love. The good news, the gospel according to Jesus, is that people are forgiven because they love God so much for loving them when they are undeserving. It's a love thing! Teaching what He commanded us is to teach:

1. God is loving. He loves the whole world. According to Paul, "God was in Christ reconciling the world unto Himself, not counting people's sins against them" (2 Corinthians 5:19). Wow! Point one is that God is not angry with sinners any more, and Jesus' life and death prove it. With this in mind, people

will love the Lord God fully, and this will meet the requirement of the Greatest Commandment—love God.

2. Love your neighbor. Love them as you love yourself. Don't enter the one-upmanship game of placing yourself above others. Show equal respect for all people as children of God and people for whom Christ died. Obviously, the minister and missionary must model this. James 2:14-17 makes this clear: "What does it profit, my brethren, if someone says he has faith, but does not have works? Can faith save him? If a brother or sister is naked and destitute of daily bread and one of you says to them, 'Depart in peace, be warmed and filled,' but you do not give them the things which are needed for the body, what does it profit?" Often Christian missions are known for sharing peace, the promise of eternal life, and not sharing what is needed for the body. We have, in this case, not truly loved our neighbors. This also needs to be done with loving humility and respect so as not to cause shame and embarrassment to the one being ministered to.

3. One last thing Jesus commanded in John 15:12-14: "This is My commandment that you love one another as I have loved you. Greater love has no one than this, that he lay down his life for his friends. You are My friends if you do whatever I command you." Love God, love your neighbor, and love sacrificially. In a nutshell, this is what Jesus has commanded us.

Disciple Making Is Making Lovers

The Great Commission is to make disciples, and the way that Jesus made disciples was to teach them to love God and to love others. The simple requirements that constitute the teaching part are these: love your neighbor as yourself, and then love that person more than you love yourself. Prove this by loving sacrificially. Love like Jesus because you are empowered by His indwelling Spirit, which is love. Too hard, you say? Remember that Jesus does not command us to do something He Himself did not do. We learned in chapter 1 that the way to have His heart is to feast on Him. We cannot imitate Jesus' love. His love is too pure, so we must incarnate this love. Act in love, expectantly knowing that the

127

indwelling Spirit will supply everything you lack. Remember that just as Braveheart had the courage of the bear, so we have the love of Christ.

What does this love look like in a person? I believe that it exceeds our idea of agape love, the unconditional love of God. American Christians tend to be accepting of those different from themselves but are rarely active in helping these hurting people. We have a mind-set of sympathy but show no compassion. This is what Jesus criticized in the Jewish leadership. Again, to quote James, we say, "depart in peace, be warmed and filled." We get all warm and comforting about the eternal bliss of heaven and how much at peace the person can be with God. We tell them to confess their sins and then they will have a right to that peace. But we often do not give them the things that are needed for the body—as James said, "what does it profit a man?"

The Compassion of Christ Empowers the Great Commission

So how does our understanding of unconditional agape love have to change to be sacrificial and active as Jesus commanded? We must add the compassion of Christ. Paul said it this way in 2 Corinthians 5:14-15: "For the love of Christ constrains us, because we judge thus; that if One died for all, then all died; and He died for all, that those who live should live no longer for themselves, but for Him who died again and rose again." What can it mean that all died? Only when we unite with Jesus, becoming one with Him, will we understand the fact that when He died, we too died. His death became our death. Dead men do not have to play the one-upmanship game. How does His resurrection apply to us? When we see ourselves as united in His death, we are also united in His resurrection. Therefore, I have given up my rights, but I have received the rightness of Jesus in their place. I live in resurrection power and love, and I have the power in His love to "resurrect" others around me. I can take a dying situation and turn it into a living one simply by sharing His love with the hurting, the neglected, and the dying. This is the compassion of Jesus, and it will compel you to act in love if you will simply die to your own ego needs and come alive in redemptive love.

Love—the Measure of Everything

The longer I live and the older I get, the more firmly I believe that love is the measure of everything in our universe. We live because God, in love, created us. We have our lives sustained because God, in love, provides for us. We became enemies of God in our minds because we were self-focused, but God, in love, restored us. We learn slowly in life that to live is to love and to love is to live, because God, in love, so created us.

The world says that love makes the world go round. I believe that God, in love, made the whole round world. There is a great picture of the God who so loved the world found in the first book of the Bible. In Genesis 1:1-3 we read, "In the beginning God created the heavens and the earth. The earth was without form and void, and darkness covered the deep. And the Spirit of God was hovering over the face of the waters. And God said, let there be light and there was light. And God saw the light that it was good." Our good God changed a dark world into a beautiful world of light in order to provide energy for every living thing.

The picture of the Spirit of God hovering over the earth is a picture of El Shaddai, the name given God that is illustrated in the female characteristic of hovering to nurture life, just as a mother hen hovers over her eggs, bringing forth the life of her chicks and later protecting the helpless chicks. This is a picture of the loving nurture of God. This is a picture of His love for all creation. We see another picture of this love in the last book of the Bible, Revelation, as it closes with a love story. In Revelation 22:17 we are told, "The Spirit and the bride say come! And let him who hears say come! And let him who thirsts come. And whoever desires let him take of the water of life freely."

It is the Spirit of God that first brought light to this world. It is the Spirit of God who says to our Lord, Jesus—come! The bride of Christ, His church, or all people related to Him, say—come! All those who hunger, thirst, and are hurting say—come! His love brought us into existence, and it will be His love that unites us together into one body as His bride for that coming complete union with Him. That, too, is love.

129

One Who Loves Must Be Exhibiting God, and Showing Forth God Is to Be Loving

In the gospel of John we learn about God's special love for His world. John 3:16 says, "God so loved the world that He gave His only begotten Son that whoever believes in Him should not perish but have everlasting life." Then the writer of the gospel of John, in a letter to the churches said, "Beloved, let us love one another for love is of God; and anyone who loves is born of God and knows God. He that loves not knows not God for God is love" (1 John 4:7).

Thus we find that love makes the world go round, and love made the world. Additionally, I have come to believe:

- Love is the creative energy that made the universe.
- Love may be the "strings" in the quantum physics "theory of everything."
- Love is the glue holding all energy in physical things.
- God is love! Love is God!
- To live is to love, and to love is to live.

Remember that Jesus commanded us to love one another as He loved us. So how did Jesus love us?

The Indescribable Love Of God

Jesus loved unreasonably:

- Expect to be told that your lifestyle is not reasonable.
- Expect to question your own sanity.
- Expect to love unexpectedly.
- Expect to love by spiritual compulsion.
- Expect to stop judging so much, because this is not loving.
- Judge not and be not judged, what do you fear?
- Expect, however, blessings you cannot now believe.

Jesus loved indiscriminately:

- Jesus loved the unlovable and ugly.
- Like Him, Mother Teresa loved the poor in gutters.
- Stop making excuses for yourself when you see a beggar. Listen to the Spirit and love.

Jesus loved consistently:
- The poor and rich, beautiful and ugly, smart and stupid, old and young, black and white, men and women, the Democrat and Republican, the straight and gay
- Love your enemies.

Jesus loved immeasurably:
- Love as if you are just like the unlimited God, because you will have His supply.
- Love as if you are invincible, because you will be in His Spirit.
- Love as if you are the only person in the world who could help, because you may be.
- Love until it feels so good when it hurts so much.

Jesus loved sacrificially:
- Love because when you give your life for your friends, you express the greatest kind of love.
- Love because God's supply never fails:
  - It is more blessed to give than to receive.
  - The more you give, the more you receive.
  - Love given sacrificially changes the recipients, and they will love you in return.

Jesus loved passionately:
- Jesus only wept twice according to the Scriptures: (1) in John 11:35 at the funeral of Lazarus and in grieving over his death—the compassion of Jesus was released over the pain of separation in death, and (2) in Luke 19:41 at the breaking of His heart over the unchanged people of Jerusalem—the compassion of Jesus was shown for people who reject truth. Do these things make us weep?

Jesus loved redemptively:
- In Genesis—God brought light to a dark world that there might be life.
- In John—God sent His son to redeem mankind.
- In Acts 10:38, "[Jesus] went about doing good and healing all who were oppressed by the devil." He healed the brokenhearted.

131

- Redemptively means to always improve from a damaged condition.
- MAKE IT BETTER!

Jesus loved with abandonment:
- Love takes risks—To love is to open yourself to being hurt—LOVE ANYWAY.
- If you love others of your gender, you may be thought to be gay—LOVE ANYWAY.
- If you love people of the other gender, you may be seen as promiscuous; be extra careful but—LOVE ANYWAY.
- If you love children, you may create concern about your being a pedophile; be careful but—LOVE ANYWAY
- If you love someone who is needy, they say you are an enabler—LOVE ANYWAY.
- If you love someone *you* need, they say you are codependent—LOVE ANYWAY.
- If you love someone who needs fixing, they will say you are a rescuer—LOVE ANYWAY.
- If you love until you drop, they say you have no boundaries; be wise but—LOVE ANYWAY.
- If you get involved in peoples lives, some will attack you—LOVE ANYWAY.
- If you love and pray for those who are ill, they may not get better—PRAY ANYWAY.
- If you fear loving unwisely because the money you give may be used for alcohol or drugs—GIVE ANYWAY.
- If you trust a friend who betrays you—TRUST ANYWAY.
- If your love seems to make little difference—LOVE ANYWAY.
- In the end we all die—LOVE AND LIVE ANYWAY!

Please understand that a person should be careful and wise, but Christians all too often let their fears keep them from compassionate love. I am not saying we should have no boundaries, become codependent or become an unhealthy rescuer. I am saying, however, that we all too often use these principles and practices to excuse our failure to love. Remember: to live is to love, and to love is to live!

Interactive Discussion Questions

1. How has the business-success motivation and the marketing methodology affected evangelicalism in this century

2. Why, do you suppose, would Jesus not leave us a model or methodology for getting someone saved?

3. What significance do you find in the fact that the Great Commandment was given before the Great Commission?

4. Do churches today tend to favor the Commandment or the Commission? Why?

5. What evidence do you have that your evangelism motive might be wrong?

6. How do unbelievers feel about most evangelicals?

7. Which is the greater good news: "If you believe like I do, you can get to heaven" or "God loves you so much that He no longer counts your sins against you"?

8. John taught, "Anyone who loves is born of God and knows God." Do you think that modern Christendom equates loving with having been born of God, or does it tend to equate being born of God with believing and confessing something new?

9. How do you relate love to the underlying power of the universe?

10. If Christians were not known as being judgmental but, instead, were seen as very loving, what difference might this make in our world?

Chapter 9
Jesus' Church – Positive or Negative?
Jesus – positive thinker

In this age of numerous choices and instant gratification, there are some in the Christian community who continually search for the perfect church much like they shop for that illusive, perfect-fitting pair of jeans. According to church pollster George Barna, 80 percent of Protestant church growth comes from transfers and biological increases. Given the fact that not many children who have reached young adulthood are staying in churches, we can deduce that the majority of adults reported in church-growth statistics are actually people who have transferred from one church to another. This is a measure of the discontent felt by many adult church members. Granted, this "church hopping" occurs most often in larger cities where more choices are available, but what is behind this increasing dissatisfaction that seems to be found everywhere?

This "just right church" has many expressions, depending on who you talk to. Some say they desire more upbeat music, while others don't like the resounding beat of the drums. Some insist on reverent worship, while others look for freedom of joyous expression. Some prefer a preacher, while others prefer a teacher-pastor. Needless to say, the list goes on and on.

These differences are evidenced in the vast array of denominations, even within sects of a denomination that vary in their understanding and expression of the Christian life. On a more basic level, we find that local, individual churches also differ based on the direction of leadership and traditions of the founders of the local church or parish.

There are many major divisions of the Christian faith. A few notable ones follow:

- Eastern Orthodox   (Western) Roman Catholic
- Roman Catholic   Protestant
- Calvinistic   Armenian (free will)
- Traditional   Pentecostal
- Charismatic   Non-charismatic
- Conservative   Liberal

135

There are, of course, many additional variations based on doctrinal differences; for example, churches that perform infant baptisms and those that will only baptize adults. At a recent count there are a reported fourteen hundred different denominations or unique brands of the Christian church. Probably there is much duplication in these if an analysis could be made to detail what they believe. I know of no such study or book, and I doubt that most of us would want to review such a detailed report. Still, we must have some means of coming to a personal peace with our choice in churches.

Bottom line: most of us join or attend a church because it meets our needs. Usually we will want the church to be aligned with our doctrines, but I have attended and even joined churches with which I had some doctrinal difference. I have a preference for the Baptist position regarding adult, believer's baptism only, but I have joined with two different churches that held to covenant theology and practice the baptism of very young children, even infants. I do not fully agree with this practice, but I find that the practice of infant baptism does not present such a negative that I could not enjoy the many positives that I found in these churches.

I personally have not experienced firsthand every kind of church listed above. I certainly have preferences on the list, but I suppose I would not refuse to attend, and maybe even join, any one of them if the options for Christian fellowship were limited because of where I lived. For example, I might attend a Catholic church if I worked in a foreign land where there was no Protestant church. There is, however, one dichotomy of Christian practice that I find of such importance that I would rather not join than to join and be continuously frustrated by it. I personally am more concerned over this difference than I am over any of the denominational differences listed above. The division I refer to is the positive-versus-negative practice of the Christian faith. The outworking of this difference can be seen as grace versus law. I contend that what most of us are actually searching for is a positive form of Christianity that is based on love and will help us to better connect with Jesus Himself as well as with others. Unfortunately, there are some churches that, although they claim to be based in grace, still teach and practice very negative forms of the faith.

I want to remind us as we approach this study that humans seem to be divided into these two categories in other ways. We know some people are pessimists and others are optimists. These two ways of approaching life seem to be fixed in human personality, both by genetics and by experience. Some people are happy and excited by life, and this seems to be a mind-set that can even be rooted in brain "wiring." Others are unhappy and depressive, and this, too, is evidenced in new scientific brain studies that show how the optimist's and pessimist's brains actually fire their neurons in differing ways.

This being the case, perhaps some of the dichotomy between positive and negative churches extends to the individual members because it may be an expression of the dominant way in which they think. Birds of a feather flock together, as the saying goes. Therefore, negative or positive religious doctrine may be an expression of the most acceptable and comfortable way in which groups of people think and feel.

Then, too, there is the matter of personal life experience. Optimistic and pessimistic approaches to life are often formed by reactions to experiences. To complicate matters, there is the phenomena of self-fulfilling prophecy. In essence, people who are prone to negative thinking often bring about their own negative experiences, or at least their interpretation of life's situations is negative. The same can be said about positive attitudes and the resulting positive experiences or interpretations of experiences. To a major degree we get what we expect, even from God. In a limited but still powerful way we co-create our own reality. Nevertheless, what evidence is there in the Bible that we should have a positive faith and a positive spiritual practice? Certainly a positive Christian faith is a much more attractive alternative when we consider our impact on our culture and community.

In this chapter I want to explore these differences and help define the way to practice a positive Christian faith. It has been suggested that a positive form of Christianity is the basis of a new reformation. It may be true that the revolution now sweeping

137

through the postmodern church (as defined by George Barna in his book, *Revolution*) will be based on this positive difference. I would suggest that to a limited degree the historic Protestant Reformation was a movement toward grace and thus was an expression of positive Christianity. The movement in the twentieth century begun by Norman Vincent Peale and popularized by Robert H. Schuller is certainly based to a large degree on positive Christianity.

The impact of positive Christian doctrine has been felt in all denominations. Unfortunately, some in the fundamentalist camp have reacted negatively to the positive doctrines and, as a result, have become further entrenched in the negative side of their Christian doctrines. Many other denominations have had some movement toward the positive form of Christian teaching and practice without being fully submitted to it. On balance, the impact of positive Christianity has been favorable to the entire Christian faith.

Positive and Negative Christianity Contrasted

What is the definition of positive Christianity, and how does it contrast with negative Christianity? The chart on the next page is my attempt to define these differences:

Positive Christianity	Negative Christianity
Presents God as love	Presents God as loving but justly wrathful
Is centered in the teachings of Christ	Places much emphasis on the Old Testament
Focuses on the grace and love of God	Focuses on the responsibility of humans
Sees humans in union with God	Sees humanity as sinful and separate from God
Presents salvation as a gift of grace alone	Presents salvation as conditioned by submission and commitment
Promotes positive self-esteem as a product of understanding our new creation in Christ	Promotes negative self-esteem by claiming mankind's condition cannot change in this life
Is love based	Is fear based
Sees mankind freed from the Law	Sees mankind as still bound by the Law

Beneath these differences lie some disagreements on the meaning of the "very words" people have chosen to express their doctrinal positions. For example, do humans have the image and likeness of God, or have they lost it due to the fall of Adam? Do the New Testament and Jesus teach the need to bring the self to death? Does this mean that the ego as defined by psychology must be crucified? When Saint Paul taught that the flesh should be crucified, is this equivalent to the self, the ego, the pre-salvation life we received from Adam? Obviously we need to find a mutually acceptable understanding of the meaning of these words before any discussion can produce meaningful results. We will, therefore, start by defining terms.

What is the likeness of God? What is the image of God?

In Genesis, mankind is said to be created in the image and likeness of God. In Genesis 1:26 God said, "let us make man in our image and according to our likeness." Later in Genesis 3:5 when Satan tempted Adam and Eve, he said they needed to eat of the tree of the knowledge of good and evil in order to be "like God, knowing good and evil." They were tempted to take something they already had! The image relates to being in the same nature as God, while the likeness relates to acting in the way God acts. One relates to the being, and the other to the doing. Image relates to the spirit, while likeness relates more to the personality or soul of man.

After the fall when the first child, Cain, was born, he was said to be in the image of Adam, meaning that he was born into the same fallen spiritual state. In Genesis 5:1-3 it says, "In the day that God created man He made him in the likeness of God," and then it says, "Adam begot a son in his own likeness, after his image." From this we see that after the fall it would be correct to say that mankind retained the likeness of God but not His image. The image of God was restored in the life and person of Jesus Christ, and only after the work of Christ (His death, burial, and resurrection) was the image of God restored in mankind. This makes humans in union with Christ into a new creation, restoring what was lost in Adam.

What Is the Self?

Jesus taught that we are to deny self. Did he mean that we must deny our own personalities? No. The actual Greek word translated into the English as "self" is *auto*. Jesus was teaching that we are not to be autonomous, acting independently from God.

What is the ego?

The word *ego* was made popular by Sigmund Freud. He defined the personality, or soul of humans, as having three parts, which he called the super ego, the ego, and the id. They are roughly like the will, mind, and emotions. They have been popularized today as the parent, the adult, and the child parts of our personalities. Ego is amoral. There is nothing wrong with the adult-level mind development the word represents. It becomes a moral issue when we refer to it as egotistical or egocentric. These words mean we have become so attached to our mental concepts that we are now

140

selfish and self-centered. In current usage the term *ego* tends to carry this negative idea.

What is the flesh?

The biblical word *flesh* has a number of usages. When the Bible says that Jesus was God in the flesh, it simply means that God became a human being. In this usage the word is amoral. Paul's use of the word *flesh* in Romans 7:18 gives a negative moral meaning. He said, "For I know that in me, that is in my flesh, dwells no good thing." Used this way, and this is the most common New Testament usage, flesh means human life apart from reliance on the Spirit of God. It means independence from God or living in the sense of separation from God. Mankind can have a positive or negative form of flesh. The positive form of flesh (humanly positive resulting in pride) is independence or separation from God, resulting in self-righteousness, while the negative form of flesh is poor self-esteem and the resulting bondage to sinful behavior.

Should Christianity Promote Positive Self-Esteem?

As a young Christian, I was warned against studying psychology and told that believers were simply sinners God saved and, therefore, were not to have high self-esteem because that led to another form of sin, pride. According to this principle, the more negative our self-image, the more spiritual we were.

I remember the words of an old hymn, "Would He devote that sacred head for such a worm as I." Indirectly I was told that believers must always think of themselves as lowly, like worms. In spite of these warnings I eventually studied psychology and theology and came to see that although excessive high self-esteem can promote pride and a haughty spirit, low self-esteem can be the source of many other forms of sin and human misery. Both can lead to separation from others and sometimes a belief that we are separated from God Himself, and both can result in human dysfunction and sin. Is low self-esteem the equivalent of humility? What is the biblical and logical balance? Did Jesus have low self-esteem? What does it mean to "esteem others better than ourselves?" Is psychology simply a manifestation of the biblical

141

prediction of people at the end of the age, "Lovers of themselves more than... lovers of God"? (II Timothy 3:2) Certainly these questions posed a real problem when related to human self-esteem and the Christian faith.

The basis of any discussion of this topic must be laid on the issue called identity. The question is, are we dignified and exciting children of God or dirty worms fit only for destruction? Has the image of God within us been so marred that humanity is destined to live at a near animal level? What is mankind's identity?

These questions form part of what is called our world-view. Actually, everyone has a world-view even if they are not conscious of it. All people live and act in certain ways because of their world-views. What is a world-view? Our world-view is how we see ourselves, life, and the whole of creation. What we believe does dramatically impact how we act. World-view, then, is a lens, much like a pair of glasses through which we see our reality. World-view is our focus on a cluster of beliefs that are central to our meaning and purpose in life.

Our world-view determines priorities, assesses meaning to events, justifies our actions, explains our relationship to God and others, and provides a context for life. It is the way we see ourselves, our identity, our self-image. When we esteem ourselves highly as creations of Almighty God, we have a positive self-image or identity. When we have a low self-image or low self-esteem, we have an accompanying negative identity and usually dislike or even hate ourselves. The result is a major consequence in the way we see creation, God, and others.

Is Our Expression of the Christian Faith Love-Based or Does It Still Promote Fear?

In 1 John 4:16-18 we read, "And we have known and believed the love that God has for us. God is love, and he who abides in love abides in God and God in him. Love has been perfected among us in this: that we may have boldness in the Day of Judgment; because as He is, so are we in this world. There is no fear in love; but perfect love casts out fear, because fear involves torment. But he

142

who fears has not been made perfect in love. We love Him because He first loved us."

In this text we see a number of things clearly presented. To begin with, it is God's love for us that came first, and we are able to love and be delivered from fear because God loved us even while we were trapped in our sins. His love is unconditional (agape), and this means that God loves sinners just as they are. Obviously, because He loves us, He wants to bring about change in us, but God's love came before our response. We can, therefore, have confidence in the coming Day of Judgment because we will not stand condemned by God for our sins.

Paul taught that "God was in Christ reconciling the world to Himself, not counting their sins against them." John concludes that God's love for us has taken away our condemnation, made the day of judgment nothing to fear, and that because of the love of God in Christ, we will never be tormented, another way of saying we will never enter hell as a place of punishment. Therefore, John says that love perfected, meaning a matured understanding of love, will cast out any fear.

This being the case, I believe the Bible teaches that when we grow up in our faith, we will come to a total peace with God (a reconciliation or unity with God) that will fill our lives with love instead of fear. When churches and Christian teachers try to return us to shame, guilt, condemnation, and fear of God, they are diametrically opposed to the teaching of Scripture on this topic. Fearless Christianity is positive Christianity and the promotion of an optimistic faith. Even if we personally struggle with a depressive personality or a history of pessimistic events, we can still submit ourselves to the unquenchable, all powerful, unconditional love of God and feel safe and at peace in His presence. His invincible love will overcome any fear if we surrender ourselves to it.

Has Christ Freed Mankind from the Law or Must Mankind Still Be Subject to the Law?

A subject closely related to love overcoming fear is the understanding of the Law in the life of believers today. In another chapter we have detailed the way Jesus fulfilled the Law but still opposed its legalistic practice. We found that love fulfills the Law, and God seeks loving rather than legalistic people to be at the forefront of His kingdom on earth. I now want to remind us about the teaching of the apostle Paul on this subject. Let these verses found in Romans, 2 Corinthians, and Galatians speak for themselves. Read them first, and then I will present a summary of what they mean.

Romans 7:4-6—"Therefore, my brethren, you also have become dead to the law through the body of Christ, that you may be married to another—to Him who was raised from the dead, that we should bear fruit to God. For when we were in the flesh, the sinful passions which were aroused by the law were at work in our members to bear fruit to death. But now we have been delivered from the law, having died to what we were held by, so that we should serve in the newness of the Spirit and not in the oldness of the letter."

II Corinthians 3:4-6—"And we have such trust through Christ toward God. Not that we are sufficient of ourselves to think of anything as being from ourselves, but our sufficiency is from God, who also made us sufficient as ministers of the new covenant, not of the letter but of the Spirit; for the letter kills, but the Spirit gives life."

Galatians 2:19-21—"For I through the law died to the law that I might live to God. I have been crucified with Christ; it is no longer I who live, but Christ lives in me; and the life which I now live in the flesh I live by faith in the Son of God, who loved me and gave Himself for me. I do not set aside the grace of God; for if righteousness comes through the law, then Christ died in vain."

It is obvious that the believer is dead to the Law, delivered from the Law, freed to serve God in the newness of the Spirit, made a sufficient minister of the grace of God, and made righteous by grace without the necessity of keeping the Law. Now I ask you, in your experience, is it not true that churches have continued to hold you and their other members to a standard of "Law keeping"? Most likely this is done out of their fear that we will all become very sinful if we are not reminded regularly about the demands of the Law.

144

Paul addresses this misdirected effort with the statement that if the righteousness God requires of us could come from keeping the Law, then Christ died in vain. Therefore, I find that negative Christianity tends to use fear and the demands of the Law as a way to manage sin. Fear and law cannot ever control or manage sin; only grace and love can.

What Difference Would It Make If We Practiced a Positive Christian Faith?

Fear only drives people away from God. Law only causes us to feel that God has demanded more of us than we can possibly produce. Negative religion, being fear based, continues to remind people of their failures and cause them to struggle in a futile attempt to please God out of their own human resources, but the flesh, the human nature without God, will always fail. Under the influence of negative religion, we fail and are whipped into an attempt to try harder, only to eventually fail again and fall further, and the result is that we become even more hopeless about ever knowing God and being in union with Him. Many helpless people who have poor self-esteem only have that self-image reinforced by the "sin, try harder, fall further" syndrome.

Now try to envision what a positive Christian faith could produce. Within the texts we quoted from the apostle Paul, we can find the answer to the self-esteem issue. To see how you can build up great self-esteem in your relationship to Christ, let's review certain parts of these three texts. In the Romans text we found this statement, "so that we should serve in the newness of the Spirit." The first hint of victory is found in the fact that the Law brings death, but the Spirit of Christ within us can give us a newness that produces life as He would live it.

The next statement, "not that we are sufficient of ourselves to think of anything as being from ourselves, but our sufficiency is from God," shows us that while we in ourselves, in our human flesh separate from God, can do nothing, we are made capable of Christ-like living by God working within us.

Finally, notice this victorious living statement in Galatians, "I have been crucified with Christ; it is no longer I who live, but

145

Christ lives in me." What failure could we ever experience if we saw ourselves as dead with Christ but made alive by His resurrection power? Would the Christ living within me ever fail to live in complete harmony with the will of God? No! Therefore it is not I who can have great self-esteem and live victoriously; it is the new I, the Theron raised with Christ, the Christ/Theron that brings about a life that will not fall short of the design of the glory of God in man.

What Scripture Endorses the Positive Christian Faith?

It is obvious that none of us ever walks in this death/resurrection new life without any error. Even the great saint, Paul, said, "Not that I have already attained but I press to the mark of the high calling in Christ Jesus." This is all that is required. We press toward the mark, the sin-overcoming life, by remaining very conscious of our being "in Christ Jesus." Then when we fail, when we walk after the flesh in opposition to the Spirit of Christ within us, we will eventually become so miserable that we will return to this perfect union with the perfect Christ, our only source of great high self-esteem and our true self-identity.

I often fail and sometimes fall, but I am already fully forgiven. Therefore I can take the failures as a powerful reminder of my absolute need to walk in tandem with Jesus Christ in the Spirit. If I am victorious, I realize that it was not my effort alone but that, as Paul said, "our sufficiency is from God." Whether I sin or whether I live as a saint, I am always and forever being reminded that I am nothing without Him and that "I can do all things through Christ who strengthens me" (Philippians 4:13).

What was God's purpose in my having His invincible Spirit contained in my flawed human life? I propose that God had a plan all along for this paradoxical paradigm. The paradox is that I incarnate Christ's perfection in my imperfect human life. This was illustrated by the apostle Paul in the 2 Corinthians 4:7-10 text, "But we have this treasure in earthen vessels, that the excellence of the power may be of God and not of us" (verse 7). This verse teaches us the reason for God's use of imperfect humans. We are only clay pots that contain the power of God, His love, and His spirit. This is so we can take no personal credit that would lead us to pride and self-righteousness. But there is another major teaching here. It is also so we will not use our own puny power source but instead will turn to His unlimited power source.

Continuing in verses 8 and 9, we read, "We are hard-pressed on every side, yet not crushed; we are perplexed, but not in despair; persecuted, but not forsaken; struck down, but not destroyed." In this text we find that we are not only simple clay pots but we will be subject to much misuse in this fallen human experience. We will be hard-pressed, perplexed, persecuted, and struck down—in other words we will experience what Jesus said we would—"in this world you will have tribulation." Then Jesus said, "but, be of good cheer, I have overcome the world" (John 16:33).

He did not say that we would be delivered from tribulation, but that His victory in this world would become our victory. While we are absolutely broken by the world's tribulation, we find that the Spirit within our clay pots (our bodies) is still victorious. We are not crushed, not in despair, not forsaken, and not destroyed. You can shatter the clay pot but you cannot put out the light shining within. That light is the Spirit of Jesus incarnate within each of us. So why must the clay pot be broken?

In verse 10 Paul also said that we are, "always carrying about in the body the dying of the Lord Jesus, that the life of Jesus also may be manifested in our body." It is simply this: We are to be broken that we might show forth the Jesus who lives in our body. Are you negative about your faith only because your life has been one of such suffering and brokenness? If so, think on this. Your brokenness can work for your own greater good. Your brokenness can have a great spiritual purpose. Your brokenness is to show forth the invincible treasure you contain. You carry about death in order that Jesus might be seen in you.

The greatest positive there is can only be found in the greatest negative of a broken life. We have found that the trials and tribulations of life are designed to break us of egotism, self-sufficiency, and self-centeredness, but we are not to remain broken and useless. These life experiences are designed to reveal what lies inside. It is the paradox that we incarnate Christ's perfection in our

147

imperfect human lives. As Paul taught us, "I can do all things through Christ who strengthens me."

Imagine what can be accomplished by the family of God in Christianity if we all see ourselves as children of the living God? What does Jesus say to us through the Scriptures? He did not then and would not now call us miserable sinners. He said that we are the salt of the earth, the light of the world, royal children of the Eternal King. He has saved us from our own defective opinions of ourselves. He has saved us for high and holy service in order that we might enjoy the dignity of our God-intended destiny. This is positive Christianity!

When the good news or gospel of Jesus is fully proclaimed, we will finally understand that we are sons and daughters of the living God. John said in 1 John 3:1a, "Behold what manner of love the Father has bestowed on us that we should be called children of God!" Then in verse 2 he said, "Beloved, now we are children of God." With this "now" mentality we can have the greatest form of self-esteem. We can esteem ourselves as perfect in Christ.

With this mind-set we can impact our culture and our world, bringing about the spiritual benefits of the kingdom of God so that Christ can reign as victor over all human failures and tragedies. We can bring about the request in the Lord's Prayer, "Thy kingdom come, thy will be done in earth as it is in heaven" (Matthew 6:10 KJV). We assist Christ in ushering in the long-awaited restoration of the image of God reigning in and over mankind. In that restored image we all find the fulfillment of our destiny, our highest level of self-esteem.

This chapter probably causes a conflict within us – we have been taught the value of brokenness and we know any form of self-esteem that leads to self-centeredness or egotism is wrong. This seems paradoxical – how can good self-esteem and brokenness be mutually integrated? In the next chapter we will see that the best self-esteem comes after the crushing of our self-centered ego. In Christian leadership this formula of brokenness first followed by the restored image of God is absolutely essential. In fact, I believe that the church Jesus envisioned must have brokenness as its foundational principle.

Interactive Discussion Questions

1. Please share your personal experience with both positive and negative forms of the Christian faith.
2. What has God taught you by experiencing some negative approaches to the Christian faith?
3. Which expression of the faith has been most attractive to you and why?
4. How does the expression of the negative or the positive Christian approach to life impact the effectiveness of our witness for Christ in our culture?
5. How might a positive approach to the faith that does not rely on the Spirit within us cause damage to our witness for Christ?
6. How does tribulation and brokenness refine our understanding of the treasure within, the Spirit of Christ?
7. Why did Paul take such care to always attach teaching about Christ living within us to his discussion of the treasure within our clay pots?
8. How do you feel about the author's position that sin and failure are parts of the divine design that drive us to dependence on the Spirit?
9. What practical steps might you take to learn to live in the balance of the divine Spirit in your vessel of clay?
10. If God has not made our humanness perfect but has chosen to place in us the perfection of the life of Jesus, what might be His reason?

Notes:

Chapter 10
Jesus Builds On Crushed Rock
Jesus' replacement, Peter

At one time or another every organization faces the problem of transition from the original leadership to a new generation of leaders. Humans grow old, retire, or die, but the organization may live on from generation to generation. The enthusiasm and vision of the founder is usually difficult, if not impossible, to match. Therefore, the selection of the second-generation leader is crucial to the long-term success of the venture.

Following a Leader Who Cannot Be Matched
Can you imagine being the follow-up leader to Jesus Christ? It may have looked like an honor, but candidly, those were difficult sandals to fill. The job description in this case also included the retirement package—the replacement leader would follow his Master to death by crucifixion. Would you want the job?

No human being would willingly volunteer for the position of being the earthly head of the church knowing what it would cost—unless death was no longer seen as a terror. There would be glory days before this final retirement, but there would also be many trials and much suffering. The job required it. When the selection of one of the Twelve was handed down by the Founder, the privilege and the passion fell on Simon Peter. What can we learn from Peter about the mystery of this spiritual-kingdom organization, and why is it so important to us as believers?

Peter, the First Second-Generation Christian Leader
Peter was an entrepreneur, a small-business owner, and a brash powerful man. We can hardly keep from liking him because in many ways he is just like us, or at least what we would like to be. I think the phrase, "open mouth, insert foot" was probably coined by the other disciples, because Peter usually spoke quickly and reactively. Even if they differed with Peter, it was not probable

151

they would have confronted him, because early stories about Peter show that he was a very strong man physically.

Peter was ambitious enough for a dozen men, and he was a bulldog when it came to tenacity. When he took hold of any project, he would not quit until it was done. Jesus probably took note of this. There was no second-place mentality in Peter. Nevertheless, Peter had his faults. He was bigger than life, but he was intensely human, too. Peter was one of us and all of us. He was the prototype of a leader for the kingdom of heaven on earth.

Peter Here, Peter There, Peter, Peter Everywhere

In his book *Bible Characters: People from the New Testament,* Dr. Alexander Whyte wrote the following description of Peter:

"The four gospels are full of Peter. After the name of our Lord, Himself, no name comes up as often as Peter's name. No disciple speaks so much and so often as Peter. Our Lord speaks oftener to Peter than to any other of the disciples; sometimes in praise and sometimes in blame. No disciple is so pointedly reproved by our Lord as Peter, and no disciple ventured to reprove his Master but Peter. No disciple ever so boldly confessed and outspokenly acknowledged and encouraged our Lord as Peter did, and no one ever intruded, and interfered, and tempted Him as repeatedly as Peter did.

"Peter's Master spoke words of approval and praise, and even blessings to Peter the like of which He never spoke to any other man. And at the same time, and almost in the same breath, He said harder things to Peter than He ever said to any other of His twelve disciples, unless it was to Judas."

Meet Simon Johnson

Peter was the son of Jonah (Barjona in the King James Version) and a native of Bethsaida, on the shores of the Sea of Galilee, a town where Jesus often spent time and taught. We have come to know him as Peter, but his given name was Simon Bar-Jonah, meaning son of Jonah. The word *Bar* meant son, so the modern equivalent of Peter's name would have been Simon Johnson.

There was nothing uncommon about the name Simon. This name was as common in Israel in that day as the name William would be to us. The history of the name traces all the way back to the sons of Jacob where Peter's namesake would have been Simeon. The names Simon and Simeon were identical and had an original meaning of "listener." Peter, however, did not live up to the name; he was a talker, not a listener.

The Listener Who Did Not Listen

The Old Testament namesake of Peter, Simeon, gave birth to a whole tribe of Israel. Simeon was mentioned with Levi in their father's blessing in a strange way. Of Simeon (and Levi) it is said that he was an instrument of cruelty and that his anger was fierce and his wrath cruel. Perhaps, in this way, Simon Peter did resemble the primary Simeon (Simon), head of one of the twelve tribes of Israel.

Peter was intensely and totally human. Peter is shown as a man of success, failure, bravado, and cowardice. His story encourages us with this fact about ourselves—we are simply clay touched by divinity. If from the story of Peter's ups and downs we can find any solace, it would be that Peter at his best became the champion of Christ only by suffering and learning through his failures at his worst.

Being what we might call hot-headed, Simon Peter was very quick to respond, usually impulsively and without much forethought. Because Peter was often the center of attention, Jesus both encouraged him and very directly criticized him. Apparently, Peter had broad shoulders and could take direct critiques.

Like that of his Old Testament namesake, Simeon, the aggressiveness of Peter was fueled by anger and wrath. Jesus saw the potential in him but also the flaw. Therefore, Jesus set out to use Peter's strength, but first had to break his will and tendency to rely on his anger for power.

Jesus was a masterful judge of men and knew about them before He got to know them. Jesus met Peter's brother Andrew before meeting Peter. It was Andrew who brought Simon Bar-Jonah (Peter) to meet Jesus. Peter and his brother Andrew had a fishing business of their own and were, from what we can learn in Scripture, successful and owned their own boat. They had entered business with two other brothers, James and John, the sons of Zebedee.

It would have been a major sacrifice for Peter to leave his thriving business to follow this homeless rabbi, Jesus. Peter, you see, owned a home in Bethsaida where he lived during the fishing season, and he also owned a home in Capernaum that, according to its description, was a larger home with a spacious courtyard that held many guests. Peter was by most standards a rich man.

With this description in mind, we can better understand the question Peter posed to Jesus in Mark 10:28. Paraphrased, it would read like this, "Look here, Jesus, we have left all our wealth behind to follow you, what do we get in return?" Is this just another brash question? No! Peter's question was justified based on what he had left behind to join Jesus in His ministry. But, there is more to this story, and we need to review it before we can see what the life of Peter illustrates about kingdom-of-heaven citizens and leaders.

Peter the Saved One, But Not Yet the Kingdom Leader

Here is, as they say, "the rest of the story," from Mark 10:23-31:

"Then Jesus looked around and said to His disciples, "How hard it is for those who have riches to enter the kingdom of God!" [Peter's ears probably perked up at this, because Jesus had just said that he, a rich man, might miss the coming kingdom of heaven.] And the disciples were astonished at His words. But Jesus answered again and said to them, "Children, how hard it is for those who trust in riches to enter the kingdom of God! It is easier for a camel to go through the eye of a needle than for a rich man to enter the kingdom of God."

"They were greatly astonished saying, "Who then can be saved?" But Jesus looked at them and said to them, "With men this is impossible, but with God all things are possible." Then Peter answered and said to Him, "See, we have left all and followed You, therefore what shall we have?" So Jesus

154

answered and said, "Assuredly, I say to you, … everyone who has left houses or brothers or sisters or father or mother or wife or children or lands, for My name's sake, shall receive a hundredfold, and inherit eternal life. But many who are first will be last, and the last first."

Peter the First Would Be the Last If He Did Not Change

This is like the good news-bad news jokes we hear today. The good news is that whatever is left behind will be multiplied and replaced, but the bad news is that it includes persecutions! In other words, having all the stuff you want will not exempt you from suffering in this world. The ultimate reward, however, comes later, and that reward is eternal life.

Character Change Follows Identity (Name) Change

Simon's name was changed by Jesus to Peter, and this is an important and interesting story, a story well worth reviewing. When Andrew brought his brother Simon to Jesus, Jesus addressed him with a very strange salutation, and in this we discover some very interesting things about Simon Peter. Within this strange three-language naming of Peter we will find out who he was in his fleshly, human nature, who he would become when his strength was refined, and why Peter, as well as all of us, had to be broken before he could be useful in the kingdom of heaven.

Jesus used three languages in his address to Peter in John 1 saying, "You are Simon the son of Jonah. You shall be called Cephas" (which is translated, A Stone).

1. Simon is a Jewish name and carried with it the potential to listen, but also the tendency to be hot-headed and angry.
2. Cephas is an Aramaic name translated "the rock."
3. Peter (or *Petros*) is a Greek name meaning a piece of rock.

It takes little interpretation of these names to see that Simon, motivated by anger, had to be broken, and that he, as the rock (Cephas), would be shattered into a stone, *Petros* (Peter).

155

Obviously rocks are thought to be stable but in his anger and wrath Peter was anything but stable.

Simon Becomes Peter, Slowly

Simon Peter was volatile, but divine grace would transform him from a violent man into a piece of the solid rock that would be useful in the kingdom of God. As a foundation stone in that new kingdom, Peter had to be solid and firm without being hot-headed and angry. Men of true courage cannot be motivated by anger. They must be motivated by loyal steadiness.

We see this name change expressed again by Jesus after Peter confessed Him as the Messiah (Christ). In Matthew 16:16 Peter called Jesus the Christ. In verses 17-18 we read, "Jesus answered and said to him, "Blessed are you Simon Bar-Jonah, for flesh and blood has not revealed this to you, but My Father who is in heaven. And I also say to you that you are *Peter*, and on this *rock* I will build My church, and the gates of Hades shall not prevail against it" (italics mine).

In this text we find that Jesus called Simon, Peter and He said that on this *rock* (*petros*, or piece of stone), He, Jesus, would build His church. I like to think that the foundation rock is Jesus Himself, and the first stone to be set in place is the confession of Peter that Jesus is the Christ, the Messiah, the chosen one from God who will set up the new and eternal kingdom of God. Peter's confession is to become the cornerstone of the church, the key confession on which all other doctrines rest.

Broken Rock Becomes the Foundation of the Church

Jesus truly is the Messiah, but this "rock" man, Peter, has much need of the Stonecutter's hammer to become fit as a cornerstone in the foundation of the church. Jesus produced a kingdom where men rule with love, not anger, wrath, or force. Peter the hot-headed angry man must become Peter the lover of men and lover of God.

It also was a defective view of the Messiah that had to be hammered into its correct shape before Peter's Messiah could be the cornerstone of the kingdom of God. What was Peter's and all the rest of the apostles' natural expectation of Christ the Messiah's role in the new kingdom?

Even after Jesus' resurrection the apostles asked Him, "Lord, will You at this time restore the kingdom to Israel?" (Acts 1:6). It is obvious that Peter and all the others continued to expect the physical overthrow of the Roman army so that the nation of Israel could have its own kingdom as it did in the glory years of King David. A quick review of these texts will show how the mindset of Peter differed from the kingdom expectations of Jesus.

Passage	Flawed Expectation	Plan of God for the kingdom
Matthew 16:22	Peter opposes Jesus' death / God planned for Him to die.	
Matthew 17:4	Peter wants to build three tabernacles / God wants Jesus only.	
Matthew 18:21	Peter will forgive seven times / God wants 490 times and more.	
Matthew 19:27	Peter wants to know his reward / Jesus wants Peter to be least.	
Matthew 26:33	Peter claims he will not fail / Jesus predicts he will fail.	
Mark 14:33	Peter sleeps / Jesus wants him awake.	
John 13:6	Peter asks Jesus not to wash his feet / Jesus says it is necessary.	

The Apostles' Expectations

The apostles wanted their version of the kingdom of God to come immediately. They wanted Jesus to become the political and social king, and they wanted Him to confront their enemies and bring down the wrath of God on them.

What did all of the followers of Jesus want from Him? They wanted to have the rule of Rome removed and the messianic kingdom to come. With this promised kingdom they expected food, clothing, health, prosperity, safety, respect, power over their enemies, and many other prophetic promises. They probably wanted a temple in every Jewish city so they did not have to make three trips a year to Jerusalem.

Three Basic Steps of Enlightenment Precede Our Kingdom Entrance

Peter's entrance into the kingdom role took three levels of commitment from him that demanded his all. Remember that Peter actually left all he had to follow Jesus, but at the point of the temptation at the trial of Jesus, Peter failed and left Jesus and returned to all he had left behind. Let's review these three steps forward and then the one backward:

- The first call of Peter was to believe in Jesus as *Savior,* the Lamb of God. At this first interaction Peter is named and defined by Jesus. Probably the miracle of turning the water into wine sealed Peter's belief in Jesus as a miracle worker who saved the party.
- The second call of Peter was to leave his business to follow Jesus for a time. In Luke 5:2 we find that Jesus called him while he was mending his nets. This call of Peter was to leave all, thus making Jesus his only Master. In Luke five we find that he and the others forsook all and followed Him. Now Jesus is presented as *Lord,* One they would follow and serve.

At this interaction Peter, Andrew, James, and John are told they will stop fishing and become fishers of men. Peter's decision was sealed when Jesus taught him a fishing lesson after a night of fishing without any success. Peter's reaction was to see his sinfulness and Christ's divinity in stark contrast. After that Peter's mother was healed of a sickness to further confirm to him that Jesus was divine.

158

- The third call of Peter was a call to further knowledge of who Jesus was. Jesus was presented as *Life* for Peter. Now instead of being motivated by anger, he will be empowered by the very life of Christ.

Understanding and Acknowledging Jesus as Savior, Lord, and Life Precedes Kingdom Living

Peter and the others were further strengthened in their faith by Jesus' making it possible for Peter to walk on the water for a few steps. Jesus then saved Peter when his faith failed. (This is predictive of the coming failure of Peter at the Crucifixion and the restoration of Peter by Jesus after the Resurrection.) Peter clearly knew that in his own life and power he was not a water-walker. On the other hand, Jesus' empowering of Peter meant that he could do all things!

I believe this was a setup by Jesus to increase Peter's courage, but Peter first had to learn that miraculous things could be done only by spiritual empowerment, not by his own willpower. At Peter's first calling, Jesus named him a rock in the foundation stone of the new kingdom. Peter's second calling caused him to see himself as a sinner in the presence of divinity. His reaction was to leave all to follow Christ as absolute Lord. Peter's third calling was an attempt to walk on water like Jesus, and this venture ended in the confirmation by Peter, "Truly You are the Son of God" (Matthew 14:33).

In the Matthew 16:16 passage we find that it is Peter who, advised by the Spirit of God, called Jesus the Christ. Thinking that Jesus was the one sent from God to rule over Israel and the nations, Peter was undoubtedly very pleased to receive the keys to the kingdom from Jesus. The absolute turn of direction came when Jesus revealed that, as Messiah, He was to die and on the third day resurrect to life. Peter's response was very normal: "Never, Lord,… this shall never happen to you!" (NIV). Jesus responded by calling Peter "Satan," hardly a way to encourage him.

"Broken Rock" Is Apt to Fail Jesus but Much More Apt to Learn Dependence on Him

159

In Luke 22:31-34 we find that Jesus predicted the denial of Peter. "'Simon, Simon, Satan has asked to sift you as wheat. But I have prayed for you (Simon) that your faith may not fail. And when you have returned to Me, strengthen your brethren'. But he (Peter) said to Him, "Lord I am ready to go with you both to prison and to death.' Then He said, 'I tell you, Peter, the rooster shall not crow this day before you will deny three times that you know Me,'"

In Luke 22:35-38 we see how Jesus actually assisted Satan in his plan to tempt Peter.

"And He said to them, 'When I sent you without money bag, knapsack, and sandals, did you lack anything?' So they said, "Nothing." Then He said to them, "But now, he who has a money bag, let him take it, and likewise a knapsack; and he who has no sword, let him sell his garment and buy one. For I say to you that this which is written must still be accomplished in Me: 'And He was numbered with the transgressors.' For the things concerning Me have an end." So they said, "Lord, look, here are two swords." And He said to them, "It is enough."

Guess who had one of the two swords? Good old Peter. With the encouragement of Jesus, don't you suppose that you, too, might have taken a swing at the high priest's servant? We find parts of the story in Matthew, Luke, and John. The men seized Jesus and arrested Him. When Jesus' followers saw what was to happen, they said, "Lord, should we strike with the sword?" (Luke 22:49). "Then Simon Peter, having a sword, drew it and struck the high priest's servant, and cut off his right ear. The servant's name was Malchus." (John 18:10).

"Put your sword in its place," Jesus said to him, "for all who take the sword will perish by the sword. Or do you think that I cannot now pray to My Father, and He will provide Me with more than twelve legions of angels? How then could the Scriptures be fulfilled, that it must happen thus?" (Matthew 26:52-54)

Please try to put yourself in Peter's place. Jesus said that Peter would be a coward and deny Christ. Jesus instructed that Peter take a sword. Peter moved very courageously to prove that he was willing to die with Jesus right there on the spot. For this act of courage Peter was chastised in front of everyone.

Peter's denials should be viewed in light of the fact that he stayed around after being totally discouraged. We will review these in Matthew 26:69-75, "Now Peter sat outside in the courtyard. And a servant girl came to him, saying, "You also were with Jesus of Galilee." But he denied it before them all, saying, "I do not know what you are saying." And when he had gone out to the gateway, another girl saw him and said to those who were there, "This fellow also was with Jesus of Nazareth." But again he denied with an oath, "I do not know the Man!" And a little later those who stood by came up and said to Peter, "Surely you also are one of them, for your speech betrays you." Then he began to curse and swear, saying, "I do not know the Man!" Immediately a rooster crowed. And Peter remembered the word of Jesus who had said to him, "Before the rooster crows, you will deny Me three times." So he went out and wept bitterly."

Can any one of us say we would have acted differently?

Next I want to address this final trial and his restoration, but first let us notice that Peter was a very big Law breaker.

Peter the Saved Apostle Is Also the Lawbreaker Supreme

Of the Ten Commandments, Peter had just broken seven. Let's review Peter's total failure under Law:

Law 1—You shall have no other gods before me: Peter's god was his human courage and his life empowered by human strength, represented by the sword.

Law 2—You shall not make a graven image. Peter's idol was the physical kingdom of Israel, not the spiritual kingdom of heaven.

Law 3—You shall not take the name of the Lord in vain. Peter swore by heaven to try to confirm to his challengers that he was telling the truth in his denial that he knew Jesus.

Law 6—You shall not murder. Peter had the intent, and I believe that if he had been a soldier and not a fisherman, he would have split the skull of the high priest's servant.

161

Law 8—You shall not steal. Peter just stole the reputation of Jesus by making Him out to be an unworthy master.

Law 9—You shall not bear false witness. Peter denied Jesus three times with false oaths.

Law 10— You shall not covet. Peter's actions were covetous because he wanted most to prove that he was worthy of being the rock and holding the keys to the kingdom. He wanted position more than he wanted to elevate and glorify Jesus.

If We Will Be Honest About It, Aren't We Just Like Peter?

Before we become too tough on Peter, let's remember that we, like Peter, are also consistent lawbreakers. Peter may have failed totally under the Law, but he was a guaranteed success: Remember that this terrible sifting by Satan was at the permission of Jesus, but the long-term faith of Peter was never in question. Jesus had already told him, "Simon, Simon, Satan has asked to sift you as wheat. But I have prayed for you, Simon, that your faith may not fail. And when you have turned back, strengthen your brethren." (Luke 22:31-32) Notice that Jesus called Peter by his old name that meant hot-headed and angry. This whole account was designed to show us that Jesus wants our maturity more than our courage.

After all of this, Peter apparently gave up on wanting to be the first pope, the rock, and the keeper of the keys, and once more decided to go fishing. It was only after this last return to the fishing business that Peter was prepared for his final calling and role as a key person in the kingdom of God.

After the resurrection Jesus would confront Peter over this failure. It is essential that we note that Jesus never even mentioned Peter's seven infractions of the Law. This, I believe, is because sin is not the issue here. The issue is Peter's faith that does not fail and his ability to love! Let's see how Jesus restored Peter after his denial and fall from grace. Remember the story of Jesus' setting the fire on the beach for a fish roast as the disciples returned to shore? Notice what He did and said in John 21:15-18.

"So when they had eaten breakfast, Jesus said to Simon Peter, "Simon, son of Jonah, do you love Me more than these?" [Jesus used the word for self-sacrificing love, *agape*.]

162

He said to Him, "Yes, Lord; You know that I love You." [Peter used the human level of friendship love *(philo)* saying he was the friend of Jesus. And what is the proof of love required by Jesus? Not a perfect life. Not obedience of the Law. Simply, love in action.] He said to him, "Feed My lambs." He said to him again a second time, "Simon, son of Jonah, do you love *(agape)*Me?" He said to Him, "Yes, Lord; You know that I love *(philo)*You." He said to him, "Tend My sheep." He said to him the third time, "Simon, son of Jonah, do you love *(philo)* Me?" Peter was grieved because He said to him the third time, "Do you love Me?" And he said to Him, "Lord, You know all things; You know that I love *(philo)* You." Jesus said to him, "Feed My sheep."

Jesus Understands We Cannot Consistently Agape Love Him and Is Content That We Are His Friends

Notice that Jesus changed His question of Peter from Do you agape me? to Do you philo me? Apparently Jesus reduced the demand of love to friendship, all the while knowing that agape love was impossible for Peter because he had not yet received the Holy Spirit, as he would at Pentecost.

How about you and me? Do we really agape love Jesus? At best, is our love only a friendship kind of love? Can we see that feeding children and caring for hurting people is more important than strict obedience to the Law?

Do You See Love as the Requirement of the Kingdom?

So what makes us think we can obey even the first and greatest commandment? Who truly loves God with all his heart, mind, soul, and strength? Like Peter, do we see that we at best are *eros* and *philos* lovers, and rarely *agape* lovers? Do we see that we cannot fulfill the Law without the empowerment of Christ to love?

This is the secret of the spreading of the kingdom of heaven. Believers must be delivered from simple self-centered love and then filled with the love of God, the love called agape. Jesus promised that He (notice He did not say *we*) would build His church—the body of people who would be changed by Jesus Himself. Water-walking promoters, like Peter, have to be crushed

163

and then raised up again to become gentle shepherds of the sheep like the Master, Jesus Christ. The church must be built on crushed rock, broken people. The question before us is, Do we prefer lamb-feeding to water-walking?

Interactive Discussion Questions

1. Jesus said of His followers contrasted to Himself, "Greater things will you do!" How does this make you feel?
2. What must come before our becoming greater?
3. Why does the greatness in the kingdom have to follow our becoming the lesser?
4. Share your rock-crushing experiences.
5. How do you relate to Peter personally?
6. Have you been so brash as to dare ask Jesus what you will receive out of your sacrifices? Why or why not?
7. Can you see that Peter was fit for eternal heaven before he was fit for the present kingdom of heaven? What does this teach us?
8. Whose mind-set do you have, that of Peter or that of Jesus?
9. If the disciples interpreted the Old Testament promises so as to have Jesus the Christ deliver them from earthly problems, how does our misconception about the reign of Jesus over us in the present kingdom of heaven compare?
10. Why, do you suppose, did Jesus in Luke 22 encourage Peter to take a sword to the Garden of Gethsemane? Is this an unfair trick or setup by Jesus?

Notes:

Chapter 11
Simply Human and Loving It
Jesus and our humanness

Recently, the fall of a prominent church leader made front-page news, and sadly, this story is not unlike many before it. In the last twenty years there has been one headline after another proclaiming the moral failure of yet another key evangelical fundamentalist leader. They come to prominence making great demands for human holiness, only to have their masks stripped from their smiling and confident faces, revealing the frightened, tortured, and conflicted children within.

Church members shake their heads and ask Why? The women weep, the male elders quickly step in to take control of the sinking ship while giving assurance that all will be well, the teenagers shrug their shoulders and admit that they do not find any real church heroes today, the pastor's children and children of the church cry over their leader/father's embarrassment, and the good wife claims that with God's help she will stick by her man – "just watch me" – as she determinedly ignores her own pain and mounting questions.

Everyone who knows him is shocked, and most are asking the same question, why would a grown man who has such prominence and power do something so foolish? But perhaps the question we should be asking is, why do we assume our leaders will be above failure and sin? Why do we assume they are different than any other Christian believer who has to deal with troubles and temptations?

The real reason for human failure is complex and cannot usually be found by asking questions of even those who know the exposed person best. The issue we all must address, leader and follower alike, is found in the statement of one fallen leader, "There is a part of my life that is so repulsive and dark that I have been warring against it all my life." We must all agree with the apostle Paul who said in Romans 7:18, "For I know that in me (that is, in my flesh) nothing good dwells".... O wretched man that I am, who will deliver me from this body of death?" (Romans 7:24)

167

The internal struggle between good and evil, the spirit and the flesh, is a part of the human condition.

Unfortunately for most of us, the fleshly self-centered ego, controlled by the child within, is not simply our innocent, damaged inner person. The inner child has a dark side. The inner child that psychology has told us about is very often not precious and wonderful, and most of us possess this flawed inner child, Paul's wretched man (the part of us that is frozen in destructive behaviors) that is simply attempting to find value and love. It was this flawed part of the Christian leader, the dark side of his damaged inner child, that he was referring to when he said, "there is a part of my life that is so repulsive and dark that I have been warring against it all my life."

Some may conclude that perhaps it is just human to be weak, repulsive, and occasionally sinful. Perhaps all attempts to be like Jesus will end in failure sooner or later. Perhaps the image of God within us is so marred by our sin that it cannot be restored. After all, as I have said earlier in this book, "we are simply clay touched by divinity," but is that all there is to the Christian life? Are we destined to a life of failure when it comes to our continuing battle with what we call repulsive sins?

I propose that the secret for spiritual victory in conjunction with human frailty can be found in the life of Jesus. It relates to His life of humanness fully surrendered to the indwelling Spirit of His Father, but there is more. It also relates to the mystery of His passion, His sufferings.

For Christ, the passion (also known by the Greek word *pathos*) came as the result of His divinity being made subject to human frailty. It was a form of suffering for God to empty Himself of His Godlike attributes and to submit to the limitations of becoming a human. The climax and pinnacle of His suffering, however, came when He became sin for us, when Jesus unjustly took upon Himself the punishment due to the vilest of sinners.

We, too, may have a form of unjust suffering or passion. This is not the suffering caused by sinful, wicked acts of a rebellious adult. In that case the suffering would be just. When do we suffer unjustly? Jesus spoke about it in Matthew 18:6, "Whoever causes

168

one of these little ones who believe in Me to sin, it would be better for him if a millstone were hung around his neck, and he were drowned in the depth of the sea."

From this text we can see that sometimes the sin of an adult individual is rooted in an act of sin performed against him when he was a child. In this case the child within becomes a shame-based child (the dark child), and these damaged emotional memories can control the actions of the adult. This passion is described in the statement, "There is a part of my life that is so repulsive and dark that I have been warring against it all my life." A rebellious sinner no longer wars against the dark side. The damaged saint who hates the sin that dwells within him is another matter. The first might be said to willfully disobey the law by an infraction, but the second acts out in a sinful manner against his own will. Paul had this struggle too. In Romans 7:20 he wrote, "Now if I do what I will not to do, it is no longer I who do it, but sin that dwells in me." Paul knew that the dark child, the damaged flesh, was not his true self. What did Paul declare as the answer? In Romans 7:24-25 Paul taught, "O wretched man that I am! Who will deliver me from this body of death? I thank God—through Jesus Christ our Lord!"

Now we are invited to return to health and freedom knowing the truth. What is the freeing truth? It is that Christ has shared our passion, our suffering over our failure, and has given us His victory with complete forgiveness for every sin. We no longer need to live in condemnation. The dark shamed child can be released.

To appropriate this freedom, we must reframe our thinking. We have a new paradigm for understanding our passion. We need to come to understand that this kind of sin is not so much a list of "bad deeds" for which we must be punished, but better described as the bad fruit Jesus used as an analogy for our failure, like a sickness within the tree. We can only become victorious over this kind of sin when we look at sin not as an infraction but instead as an infection. It is not a sin that stems from a heart attitude of hate, but sinful acts that flow out of a broken heart like an oozing infection. The infraction *has been* fully forgiven by God who no longer holds mankind's sins against them. Paul taught that in

Christ the Law has been fully satisfied. The infection, however, *is the continuing power* these memories of past sins holds against us when we submit to the lies of self-condemnation. We need to be transformed and no longer bound by shame and condemnation.

Paul instructed us to be transformed by the renewing of our minds. The word he used for mind involves our total soul, our whole self. It involves not only what we think but what we feel. We have been fully forgiven, so sin has no power to condemn us, but we have yet to be transformed. Transformation comes when we reach the stage where the memories of our past sin and failure have no power over us today. We find peace and victory when we place the Cross and passion of Christ between our past memories and our current temptation.

How is this infection cured? The answer is found in the word *wholeness*. Wholeness is holiness, but for human beings, holiness will never be sinlessness. We always fall short of the glory of God, often because we are simply limited humans. Therefore, we will find some level of sin (falling short of God's glory) in every action. Holiness relates to the Hebrew word *shalom*. Shalom can mean peace, but the peace comes from wholeness. The human condition, however, is fractured. We all want to be fully glorious, godlike beings, but we find we are forever much less. Our spirits have been united with the Holy Spirit so that we are complete and holy in Christ; still, our souls and bodies have yet to be redeemed and purified.

We must recognize that our treasure is in earthen vessels. This is the paradigm of our humanness containing divinity. So how do we handle this suffering, this recognition of our failure to be all we were designed to be? We find that some simply deny the dark side of themselves. They refuse to acknowledge that it exists because it doesn't fit with their theology. It doesn't fit the "good Christian" model taught by the church. Some even go so far as to present the church as a group of Christians who are sinless, well adjusted and whole. However, when Christian leaders have attempted to present themselves this way, usually God has made sure their artificial masks got stripped away. These pretenses at human holiness without the pathos or passion of struggle with sin result in eventual

170

failure by those who pretend sinlessness. The unreal standard also sends many suffering people away from the church, still feeling separate, lonely, and hopeless because they are not perfect.

What all of us have in common, leader and follower alike, is our pathos, the suffering experienced because of our struggle with our own sin and failure. Being honest and open about that is the gateway to healing. We can gladly receive the healing from the passion of the Christ when we hear Him say, "In the world you will have tribulation;" [I would say this includes our struggle with our passions] "but be of good cheer, I have overcome the world" (John 16:33).Notice that Christ's answer was not that Christians must do something when facing the struggle with their dark inner selves. His answer was that He had already overcome the world. How do we appropriate this? There are two distinctly different ways to approach this problem—the religious way and the spiritual way. In religion, people attempt to please God, others, and themselves by their devout practices; but if we are spiritual, we can rest in the fact that the battle has already been won. In the statement, "There is a part of my life that is so repulsive and dark that I have been warring against it all my life," we find a religious rather than a spiritual paradigm revealed. Paul and Jesus recommended a different paradigm, or way of looking at this problem, one in which the war is over and we rest in the victory of Jesus.

In their approach to the Christian life, people respond either with religion or true spirituality. Those who practice religion attempt to live in such a way as to please God and to make others respect them, and they often make a pretense of being sinless. Spirituality, however, allows us to live in the reality of our humanness and its weaknesses, trusting in our forgiveness when we fail. On the other hand, when we succeed, it is because we are receiving the life and Spirit of Jesus as the power to keep us above sin and failure moment by moment. Slowly we learn to hold on to this mystery of "clay touched by divinity." We learn that it is acceptable to God to be simply vessels of clay that contain the treasure of the Spirit.

Paul tells us that, "We have this treasure [of the Holy Spirit] in earthen vessels that the excellence of the power may be of God and not of us" (2 Corinthians 4:7). The problem for most of us is that we place emphasis on either our divine connection or our broken clay vessels and cannot find a balance integrating both of them. This leads to our "infection," the unhealthy split within us whereby we reject a part of our selves.

What is the result of this denial of the dark, damaged child within? We develop two lives, one in public, especially at church, and one in private when no one is looking. Now it is true that we must reject the *behavior* of the dark child, but we do not need to reject the child. The child is a part of us. Unfortunately, we throw out the baby with the bath water, so to speak. We reject the dark side of ourselves, and this makes the split within us more painful and prominent. This leads to more hypocrisy because we must pretend to be something we are not. What does Scripture say about this split? In James 1:8 we find, "A double-minded man, unstable in all his ways." The word translated "double-minded" is, in Greek, *di-psuchos,* or double souled. This means that all of us to some degree have at least two personalities (souls). No wonder we are so unstable.

This double-mindedness results in most of us trying to manage the sin in our lives, but we do not come to healing. Healing would reunite the split within our personhood. We must enfold the dark side as a part of our total selves without endorsing the behavior of the dark child within. This is not unlike loving your own child while punishing her for her actions. If the sinning child even gets a hint that she is shameful and wicked, it will scar her for life. No! The child is wonderful and loved, but the action is wrong. This makes the child to blame for her sin but not shamed for sinning. It has been said that blame means we do something wrong, but shame means that we ourselves are wrong. This internal shame that has been falsely assigned to the dark child within is our problem.

My years of counseling have taught me that the emphasis on legalism and moral regulations in the modern traditional churches produces shame by placing the emphasis in the wrong place. By always talking about what we should do, we set up an unreasonable expectation and then fail to just live as we were designed to live. But this problem has a solution that is also found in the unique life of Jesus. The argument goes like this: Jesus was unusual in that He was 100 percent God and 100 percent man simultaneously. He could not have been 50 percent God and 50 percent man because, in that case, He would have failed to be fully God, fully man. This marvelous mixture is called the hypostatic union.

Believers Also Are a Hypostatic Union of God and Man

What if the Christian believer is to be just like Jesus in this respect also? What if we are a marvelous mixture of humanity and divinity? It is true if we consider that we are to incarnate Christ, as we learned in the first chapter. The Christ in me is 100 percent divine, and the Theron in me is 100 percent human. Right? Let me say this carefully.

In theology the word hypostatic has a limited and special meaning. It describes the unique makeup of Christ. In this usage only Christ can be described as having a hypostatic (100% human and 100% divine) nature, and He is the only 'God–man' in this sense. In science, however, the word is used with a much broader meaning. Webster's dictionary says that hypostatic means "having to do with substance or essential essence" and "something masked by another thing".I am using it in the scientific sense, so I hope that those trained in theology will bear with me.

In counseling I have found that when believers sin they cannot see themselves as perfect or complete in Christ. How can they have His righteousness and act in unrighteousness? The answer lies in understanding our new spiritual nature which is housed in or masked by our human fleshly failings. We call this spiritual identity our true identity.

What are we essentially as new creations in Christ? Jesus made this very simple to see. John 3:6 says, "That which is born of the flesh is flesh and that which is born of the Spirit is spirit." If we have received the Spirit of Christ, we have become one spirit with Him. And in 1 Corinthians 6:17 we read, "But he who is joined to the Lord is one spirit with Him." Essentially, if you are born from above you are not flesh but spirit. Do we know and live by this new identity in Christ?

Think of our hypostatic union this way. Believers are spirit beings primarily, but our flesh (skin) makes us think we are only physical beings. We are not physical beings having a spiritual experience, we are spiritual beings having a physical experience.

But, I do not live easily with this tension. I struggle enough with simply dealing with my humanity. In my own life, my early years were dominated with trying to discover my identity as a human being and how I was designed to live. Slowly, and sometimes painfully, I began to understand who I was and the uniqueness of my personality. Then I met and came to know this person named Jesus. I so admired Him that I wanted to be just like Him.

The problem was that I also liked being Theron and had struggled for years, against much opposition, to become the unique me. I didn't want to lose my "Theron-ness" in the process of becoming Christ-like. I was not willing to give up that hard-earned identity to become a Christ-one. On the other hand, I was aware that the Christ-like Theron would be a better person.

This caused me to flip back and forth from an emphasis on my hard-earned identity as a human to an emphasis on my new identity in Christ. We know that the Bible calls the controlling emphasis on self, on Theron being Theron, the flesh. We also know that the Bible calls the new man in me my spiritual identity. Thus, the battle, according to St. Paul, is a battle within us between the flesh and the spirit.

In this battle of flesh and spirit, many believers deny their humanness in an attempt to shed the flesh, their sinfulness. We simply get confused between what is flesh and what is human. Jesus never expected this. His hypostatic union, 100 percent God and 100 percent man, is our model. Only when empowered by His loving nature can we become fully human and yet fully spiritual.

Accepting and Living Life

I believe it is time for most of us to end this black-and-white struggle. We have become entranced by the process of judging things black or white, good or evil, flesh or spirit. The struggle between the flesh and the spirit returns us to that ancient and awful tree called the tree of the knowledge of good and evil, and that tree only produces death.

There was another option in the middle of the Garden of Eden, and it was called the tree of life. This tree produced eternal life. If you feasted on it, you would live forever. This makes me think of a song John Denver used to sing, "Sweet Surrender." Do you remember some of the lines? "Sweet, sweet surrender, live without care, like the fish in the water, like the birds in the air." Can you imagine a fish having to stop swimming in order to think about what a fish should act like? Can you imagine a bird stopping in mid-flight to wonder if it is flying correctly? That would be utter nonsense! Fish automatically have "fishness" and birds automatically have "birdness," so they simply act as they are without any worry about failure.

Those two trees in the Garden of Eden are still with us as human beings. Unlike the fish and birds, we are stuck with this thing called knowing. Our downfall came with the "knowledge" of good and evil. Mankind lost its innocence and stopped simply being, having become cursed with the knowledge that everything, including our actions, might be good or evil. And this happened to Adam and Eve, as well as to every adolescent person who is their offspring. Babies, you see, are content to simply be who they are, and it is only during the aging and maturing process that they become self-analytical. It was perfectly natural and all right for me to wet my pants when six months old. It wasn't my problem! Then my parents had to tell me that I could no longer do that. I was told that I was a good little boy if I went in the potty, but a bad little boy if I went in my pants.

I now had a concept of the knowledge of good and evil, and as I matured in knowledge, my life was ruled and controlled by more laws and adult expectations. I tried so hard to be all that my parents told me I should be. I was fortunate my parents were loving and lenient with me. I had fewer rules and expectations than most kids. Still, at that magical time called the teen years, I rebelled and said, "enough is enough." I wanted to be my own boss for a while. I bet that at some level you did too. Symbolically, we all ate one of the apples from Adam and Eve's tree. In the process of becoming an independent and unique individual, every one of us started judging fruit. We became our own judge of what is good and what is evil, and something inside of us just died.

Duality, Judging Between Good and Evil, Ends in Death

What happened to Adam and Eve when they ate of the tree of the knowledge of good and evil? First they saw themselves as naked. Heaven forbid! God created them this way, and they were perfectly okay with nakedness until the fruit of that forbidden tree caused them to ask the question, "Is it good or evil to be naked?" Not being sure, the first thing they did was to clothe themselves in leaves. Questions, questions, questions! Should we use grape leaves or fig leaves, or perhaps palm fronds? What would our parent, God, expect?

Happening number two—they hid themselves for fear the clothing thing might not be acceptable to God. And we human beings have been struggling with these two things for thousands of years. Recognizing our nakedness and becoming self-conscious, we felt shame and hid ourselves. Actually, believe it or not, we are all naked underneath our clothing! So, the clothing thing is not really the solution, is it? When confronted by God about the disobedience of eating from that awful tree, Adam blamed Eve, and Eve blamed the serpent who beguiled her, and that is the final piece of the puzzle. We become self-conscious, we recognize our nakedness, we cover up and hide in our shame; next, we blame others; and we finally end up blaming God who created us like this. Is there a better way? For sure!

Jesus died naked on a tree. That was to be the end of the tree of the knowledge of good and evil. This tree represents the Law. The Law required death to the one who ate of it. Jesus took that death for us and directed us to another tree, the tree of life. Now we can sing a different song, "Sweet, sweet surrender, live without care, like the human part of Jesus, like His spiritual breath of air." Would you like to simply live in union with Him and knock off this eternal judging of good and evil?

176

You Are a Human Being, Not a Human Doing, So Just Be!

Jesus, you see, was never troubled with how to live. For Jesus, to live was simply to express the will and Spirit of His Father. He said it often, as in John 14:10, "Do you not believe that I am in the Father and the Father in Me? The words I speak to you I do not speak to you on My own authority; but the Father who dwells in Me does the works."

I want to put myself in the place of Jesus and paraphrase John 14:10: "You better believe me, I am in Christ and Christ is in me. We are so united that we work in tandem. I live on the basis of what He has told me, and this is my authority for living as I do. This extends to my very action or works. They are not mine but are produced by Christ in me." Do you see this?

But any person might ask, "What are the words I should speak and the works I should do?" Again we turn to Jesus who expressed His answer to these questions in John 6:28-29, "Then they said to Him, 'What shall we do to work the works of God?' Jesus answered and said to them, 'This is the work of God, that you believe in Him whom He sent.'"

Wonderful words! Our work is to believe, and the right results will follow. But, we might ask, what belief leads to the work of God? In the verses that follow the people asked Jesus what sign would be given that they might believe on Him and produce these good works. They reminded Jesus that Moses had produced bread from heaven (manna) to eat so that the people might believe. Jesus said to them, "'Most assuredly, I say to you, Moses did not give you the bread from heaven, but My Father gives you the true bread from heaven. For the bread of God is He who comes down from heaven and gives life to the world.' Then they said to Him, 'Lord, give us this bread always.' And Jesus said, 'I am the bread of life'" (John 6:32-35a).

I know I desire physical bread, but I really need spiritual bread. This spiritual bread from heaven is the body of Christ. We learned earlier that when we take communion, the spiritual purpose is that we might ingest the body of Christ in order that we might have His very nature. Communion is the reminder of my incarnation of the very life of Christ. He was given to me for this purpose. This is the

177

work God gave me to do, to walk out my life in constant tandem with Christ, knowing that Christ now lives in me, as me.

God Is Our Source of Being, Christ in Me the Hope of Glory

Another way to see this truth is found in Matthew 5:16, where Jesus said, "Let your light so shine before men that they will see your good works and glorify your Father in heaven." From what source comes my light? Again I paraphrase, "Christ is in me, and I am in Christ; therefore the spiritual essence of Christ being seen as light is now in me. When I act or do my works, they are actually coming from my light source, Jesus. This is necessary that I not be proud of my good works, because I know they are actually the product of Christ living in me, as me."

Now let us look to the text in Ephesians 2:8-10: "For by grace you have been saved through faith and that not of yourselves; it is the gift of God, not of works lest anyone should boast. For we are His workmanship created in Christ Jesus for good works, which God prepared beforehand that we should walk in them."

One final personal paraphrase, "My salvation was simply a gift given to me at the crucifixion and resurrection of Christ. I could not arrange my own salvation, obtain permanent forgiveness of all my sins, or receive eternal life that produces resurrection from the dead. All of this was given to me without any effort on my part *because it was done about two thousand years ago.* The purpose, however, was that I should do the work of God, perform certain destined good works. As I believe this, I find it happening. It is effortless but also very effective. This is what Jesus promised—His burden is light. "Sweet, sweet surrender—live without care," because my life in Christ is already finished, destined to God's design from before I was born. I am simply to enjoy the experience of this life walk with Christ."

But a question still arises, what about our temptations to sin? Must we not judge possible consequences as good or evil and then try with all our might to avoid the evil? Well, yes and no. As a child we had to learn the difference and be taught to obey. The Scriptures are thus filled with many warnings and many things we are supposed to do or not do. This is because in those instances it is

178

speaking to spiritual children rather than spiritual elders. It would be incorrect for us not to set standards of good behavior and punishment for children. It is, however, necessary to give different instruction to mature saints.

For example, I know that a good parent would not say to a two-year-old, "Honey, I love you and want to teach you about the freedom of grace. I will let you go and play in a busy street if you want to." No! Obviously the child has no concept of the risk presented in the busy street. We must, in love, tell the child not to enter the street on the basis that disobedience will result in a prompt spanking. So it is with physical and spiritual children. However, we should eventually be able to put away the childish things. But I am afraid we do not.

Putting Away Childish Things

We Christians, as well as most leaders of the church, continue to rely on the techniques we used for children, "avoid going into the street." The problem with this, however, is that if we try to avoid the temptation to sin, we never can experience spiritual victory. I want to say this very carefully because young Christians must avoid the temptation to sin, just as the child must avoid the street, but avoiding sin as mature adults (those who are learning, or have learned, to live from our spiritual resources in Christ) means that we often fail to fully live and fully love.

Battles avoided are never battles won. The time comes when we must face our demons and our own selfish flesh. Remember, Jesus did not say to overcome evil by avoidance. Jesus said to overcome evil with good. This is why I believe that the mature saint must face the evil and face his or her own selfish flesh, and then enter the very middle of the battle by loving through the temptation. Love, you see, not only fulfills the law, it changes selfish behavior and dissolves away evil.

Seeing Sin Not So Much as a Failure but as a Life Lesson

We mature in Christ when we understand sin at a new level. We ask the question, why did God allow for sin anyway? What is its purpose? At spiritual maturity we will discover that sin is the lesson; love is the answer. Every time we give in to sin, allow evil to win, or choose to walk in the flesh, there is pain and suffering. Slowly, we see that sin has a purpose of returning us to the path of love, the pathway taken by Christ. Then, we can say, "My work is to believe that the Christ life in me (always manifesting in love) can overcome any sin, win over evil, and direct me from self-centered fleshly living to victorious spiritual living." Sin, flesh, and evil always bring death, but loving always produces life. To live is to love, and to love is to live.

God designed our humanness and called it good. There is nothing wrong with us, even in our nakedness, if we will walk as we were designed. We are not designed to live in independence from God but, instead, in total dependence upon Him. We are not to see ourselves as separate from God and other people—we can stop hiding like Adam and Eve. Separation is the result of sin and the consciousness of sinfulness. We were reunited with God by the death and resurrection of Christ. We were also vitally reconnected to other people by becoming one with them in the body of Christ. Finally we can live a life of connectedness and love. This life of love fulfills the commandments, exceeds the demands of the Law, and overcomes the curse of death. When we live because He lived, we love because He loved, and then we are no longer under sin's power. It was love that paid for our sins, and it is love that delivers us from our sins. All sin is simply the lack of love.

Now, in summary, how can we apply this to the plight of the fallen pastor? The statement he made that we have repeated was, "There is a part of my life that is so repulsive and dark that I have been warring against it all my life." Usually that twisted part evolved from childhood hurts.

The rejection of his humanness is seen in his apparent inability to admit that he was a human male who had repulsive and dark sexual needs. This led to his keeping the struggle secret. The result of the secrecy was the development of the split between his spiritual self and that part of his life he called repulsive and dark. He was, therefore, rejecting himself, not just his sin, and this multiplied his shame. If he had accepted himself fully, including his powerful sexual temptation, he could have talked openly about the struggle with a counselor or some people in his church and eventually found healing. The book of James advises us to, "Confess your trespasses to one another and pray for one another that you may be healed." (James 5:16) This verse does not say we must simply confess to God. Our healing follows our transparency with other people.

Additionally, his statement gives a clue as to why he failed. He said, "I have been warring against it." There is no better formula for failure than attempting to win in our own strength. The battle for the believer, according to Paul, is spirit against flesh. We are believers, and our spirit includes His Spirit because we are spiritually one with Christ. Therefore, victory comes when we let the Christ in us control our actions. This means that we must be totally transparent with Christ as well. It does us no good to cover ourselves and hide as Adam did. There is no shame for the believer because God no longer condemns us. We can come out of hiding and be healed by becoming spiritually naked.

Shame and condemnation cause us to call ourselves "repulsive and dark" when we are actually light in the Lord. The personal confrontation of the actions of the damaged dark child within must be done gently. If we get too fierce and angry with ourselves, our hearts close and split the child away from the rest of our self. Paul said, "it is no longer I who do it [sin], but sin that dwells in me" (Romans 7:17, 20). Our problem is that we identify our true selves with the actions of the dark, damaged child. In identifying ourselves with the dark child, we reject not simply the action of sin but also the damaged child within. This simply increases our shame, further trapping us in this false identity. This poor pastor actually saw himself as the repulsive dark one, and that repulsive one continued in dark and repulsive behavior.

Paul's answer to overcoming our passion of internal conflict is found in Romans 8:1 where he said, "There is therefore now no condemnation to those who are in Christ Jesus, who do not walk according to the flesh but according to the Spirit." In Galatians 5:16 Paul also said, "Walk in the Spirit and you will not fulfill the lust of the flesh." Notice he did not say to stop walking in the lust of the flesh. Concentration on the fleshly failure only makes it worse. His command is positive because only the Spirit of Christ within can give us victory. He asked, who can rescue us, then said, "I thank God—through Jesus Christ our Lord" (Romans 7:25).

Have you come to holiness, to wholeness? Do you see yourself as perfect and full of light in the Lord? Can you reject the actions caused by "The sin that dwells in us" without calling your true identity one who is "dark and repulsive"? Can you invite Jesus to walk with you through the next temptation? If not, will you become fully transparent with someone as soon as possible?

Interactive Discussion Questions

1. How does the failure of church leaders make you feel?
2. In addition to the sorrow we feel over Christian failure, what encouragement might we find in their struggle?
3. Have you had a struggle with your own dark side? If appropriate, can you share your spiritual faults?
4. Does being an earthen vessel of clay touched by God cause you frustration or joy? Why?
5. Is there a part of your life that you keep hidden in shame? Can you distinguish between being to blame for acting in sinful ways without being shamed and rejecting yourself? If you can't answer yes, why not? (If necessary, feel free to say you aren't ready to address this with others, but do try to find someone you trust with whom you can discuss it.)
6. What might be the result if you could enfold your dark-child side?
7. If churches helped people to be whole as spiritual beings who are also weak humans, how might this manage sin in a different way?
8. Why might we as church members feel we must control sin?
9. Is our thinking controlled by fear or by love?
10. Are you stuck in the tree of the knowledge of good and evil? What is the result?
11. How would you be different if you ate consistently of the tree of life?
12. What would it take to embrace your Christ-likeness? Would you lose your humanness?
13. How might seeing yourself as an incarnation of Christ change your thinking and behavior?
14. Which tree must we start out in, the Tree of the Knowledge of Good and Evil or the Tree of Life? Why?

Notes:

Chapter 12
Jesus' Reign – 2000 Years and Counting
Jesus and blessedness

I have been very blessed to have had the opportunity to share the message of this book with you. Some of the dilemmas presented have gnawed at me for years, but during those years as I researched and prayed about them, God unfolded the beautiful truths about our freedom in Christ that I've shared with you. I am very hopeful this book has been a blessing in your life as well. I know our heavenly Father is honored when we bless His Son, Jesus, by focusing our hearts on Him. This is the way of personal blessing—we give, and it just keeps cycling back to us. We bless others, and we ourselves are blessed in the process.

The Mystery of the Kingdom of Heaven

You may wonder why I undertake to reveal the blessed, or happy, kingdom of heaven in this last chapter. I know the blessed-kingdom concept is not often discussed or taught. In fact, any major emphasis on what Jesus meant when He taught about the kingdom of heaven is unusual in today's church culture, except as a "place" we enter after death. Perhaps it's because it is sometimes difficult to comprehend. One example is that the phrases "kingdom of heaven" and "kingdom of God" are sometimes used interchangeably in the New Testament. We see evidence of this when Matthew and Mark each give their individual accounts of the same teaching by Jesus to the disciples about the difficulty for a rich man to enter the kingdom (see Matthew 19:23 and Mark 10:23). But more likely it's because our Western culture has cultivated a fear of anything mysterious, unseen, or spiritual, and this is especially true in many of our churches. Spiritual truths are taught from a rational perspective, but spiritual experiences are approached and examined with skepticism and doubt. However, I believe with all my heart that the truth about the kingdom of heaven is a missing link between the logical and the experiential levels of spiritual reality for most believers in our era.

As we look more closely at this topic, you will not follow my teaching or grasp its significance if you think of the kingdom of heaven only as a place where believers go after they die. Nor will it make sense to you if you expect that the kingdom of heaven will become reality only upon the return of Jesus to reign from Israel in some future millennial reign. I believe, as you will see, that the primary teaching of Jesus about the kingdom of heaven is for us right now. It is a way of spiritual living, a different way of seeing life. It is greater than the church or any political kingdom on earth. The kingdom of heaven is a transcendent realm above all the suffering and pain of this world, and this is one of the reasons it is called blessed.

How would you define blessedness? This is a seldom-used word today, except for the silly way we say, "Bless you!" to a person who just sneezed. When we pray before a meal we say we are blessing the food. But I am afraid these common uses fall far short of the power in the word *blessing*. Perhaps we mean by blessing the sneezer that we are pleased he didn't sneeze on us. Perhaps by saying that we bless the food, we are simply saying we give thanks for it. Of the two uses, I believe that thankfulness best relates to blessing. What, then, is a biblical blessing?

Being Blessed by Being Kingdom Aware

The Greek word for "blessed" is *makarios*, meaning "supremely fortunate, well off, happy, blessed, or to beatify." There may be many kinds of spiritual blessings, but the primary meaning comes from the concept of inheritance. You will probably remember that the blessing of the largest part of an inheritance fell to the oldest son, according to Jewish law. Blind, old Isaac had two sons, Esau and Jacob. Esau was the one who was to get the blessing of inheritance with the highest favor. Jacob and his mother tricked Isaac into giving the blessing to Jacob at Esau's expense.

In a similar way, we inherit the kingdom from our Father, God. The blessing and right to inherit rightfully belonged to our older brother, Jesus, but He graciously died that we might receive it instead. It was the good pleasure of the heavenly Father to give us this highest favor due only to His Son, Jesus. The prophecy in

Isaiah said that it pleased the Lord God to bruise Him. God was pleased to allow His Son to die for us, not only for payment for our sins, but also that we might share in the inheritance that only Jesus rightfully deserved. What an inheritance this is! We have His righteousness, His eternal life, His resurrection power, and His glory shared with us, even when we are the undeserving younger siblings.

Certainly we are blessed to be invited and even empowered to enter this special kingdom. We know that God wants all people to enter this realm and to receive the blessings that kingdom citizenship entails. In Luke 12:31-34 we read, "But seek the kingdom of God and all these things will be added to you. Do not fear, little flock, for it is your Father's good pleasure to give you the kingdom.... For where your treasure is, there your heart will be also." Jesus let His little flock of followers know that God was delighted to offer them the kingdom of heaven.

Our Religious Views and the Kingdom of Heaven

Columnist and humorist Dave Barry once said, "People who want to share their religious views with you almost never want you to share yours with them." Isn't it interesting that most people are so narrow as to believe they have the only and complete truth? Part of the reason for our narrowness is that we emphasize what we believe in our particular church and do not even think about the greater issues of the kingdom of heaven. For this self-centered reason we find that the more persistent the form of evangelism to a limited concept of truth, the more the evangelical's fervor in making a proselyte of others.

Jesus criticized this practice of the Pharisees, and I am sure He would be critical of evangelical fundamentalism (in any religion) today. Here is what He said in Matthew 23:15: "Woe to you, scribes and Pharisees, hypocrites, for you travel land and sea to win one proselyte, and when he is won, you make him twice as much a son of hell as yourselves." In this day when we live in a world-wide village because of television, books, and especially cyberspace, it is necessary to at least have a heart attitude that

187

accepts, or even favors, diversity and is not intolerant of other belief systems.

We talk a lot about church, about ministry, and about what we believe, but do we seek with passionate hearts to enter and live in and from the kingdom of heaven right now? If your reaction is to think that the kingdom of heaven is only entered when a person dies, or if you think that the kingdom of heaven, the reign of God on this earth, must wait the return of Christ at the Rapture or the end of a terrible tribulation—I have very good news, yes gospel level news, for you! Jesus connected the gospel directly to His teaching about the kingdom of heaven.

Jesus used the phrase "the kingdom of heaven" (or kingdom of God) eighty times in the four Gospels. What is so significant about that? Jesus taught regarding the kingdom of heaven:

- five times more than He spoke of hell;
- four times more than He spoke of money;
- three times more than He spoke of sin; and
- two times more than He spoke about love.

For Jesus, the kingdom-of-heaven message was essential to the gospel message, and it was His main theme. In fact, for Jesus, they were one and the same message. We find them combined in Matthew 4:23: "Now Jesus went about all Galilee, teaching in the synagogues, preaching the gospel of the kingdom."

The Unseen Spiritual Kingdom Is the Present Manifestation of the Kingdom of Heaven

Jesus also taught that the kingdom of heaven was already on earth in His time; this is good news. Better yet, you do not have to travel to Israel or some other part of the world to enter the kingdom of heaven. The kingdom is as close as the air you are breathing. The kingdom of heaven cannot be found by physical observation, but the kingdom of heaven is, nevertheless, already here with us and very healthy and thriving.

Jesus said it this way in Luke 17:20-21: "The kingdom of God does not come by observation. Nor will they say, 'See here!' or 'See there!' For indeed the kingdom of God is within you." From this we can learn that this special realm is not a physical place we can observe; it is a spiritual realm that exists not only among us but in each of us.

It was for this reason, as we have already seen, that Jesus predicted and foresaw the destruction of the physical temple in Jerusalem. It was for this truth that Jesus taught the Samaritan woman at the well that the people needed no building or special place to worship, because God was seeking persons who would worship Him in this spiritual realm.

It was for this reason that the apostle Paul taught clearly in 2 Corinthians 3:16, "Do you not know that you are the temple of God and that the Spirit of God dwells in you?" He went on to teach that we should not defile our bodies, because that would be the equivalent of defiling the temple. Jesus also taught in John 14:23, "If anyone loves Me, he will keep My word, and My Father will love him, and We will come to him and make Our home in him."

Where the Kingdom Is, There Is Jesus; and Where Jesus Is, There Is the Kingdom

Nothing could be more clearly defined than this: the kingdom of heaven (God) is an internal, spiritual kingdom residing in us and is the means of bringing the triune God into our lives. But how can you seek it with all your heart if your heart is directed toward a future physical kingdom? How can we desire a physical kingdom without reducing our desire for the spiritual kingdom realm? I am afraid we are seeking what we already have, much like Adam and Eve sought to be like God (as the serpent promised) and thus ate of the tree of the knowledge of good and evil. I want you to note that Adam and Eve were created like God. They already had what Satan tempted them to strongly desire and independently attempt to attain.

We now know that the inheritance of the kingdom of heaven came at the expense of Jesus, our older brother. We have probably seen the movie *The Passion of the Christ* or read about Jesus' suffering and death on our behalf. We know this was suffering beyond description, and it qualified Jesus for the title "Man of sorrows." The Scriptures also reveal that Jesus went through this hell on earth, enduring it for the joy set before Him—the joy of

189

sharing this gift with you and me. But, I wonder if we also know that this same Jesus was the happy Messiah who reigns from His blessed (happy) kingdom?

The Beatitudes taught by Jesus in Matthew 5:1-12 are blessings people receive when they spiritually see and experientially enter the realm known as the kingdom of heaven (God). Jesus won the right to be King of kings. He inherited this place of honor and power from His heavenly Father, and then He gave it to us. Now we can rule with Him and for Him from the place of power—from the kingdom-of-heaven realm.

If We Miss Sovereignty, We May Well Miss the Kingdom

In every kingdom there is a king, there are citizens, and there are rules and benefits. These factors are also keys to understanding the kingdom of heaven. First, there is the King, and He is Jesus Christ the Lord. He inherited the role of King because He is the firstborn, only begotten Son of the Father who is the source of all that exists and whose sovereignty extends to all things, including this heavenly, spiritual kingdom. We are most blessed, most blissful, most happy when we submit to the vision of Christ's kingdom rule.

Kings by definition are sovereigns. They rule absolutely. So it is with God the Father and with His Son and appointed king, Jesus. We do not properly understand the sovereignty of God in our generation, partially because we do not understand sovereign control. We live in a democracy, so we think of the rule of the people. Such a concept was almost unheard of in biblical times, because kingdoms and kings were the common form of government. Citizens had some rights but only as they submitted to the authority of the ruler.

Citizenship in a kingdom was a special right. There were many people dwelling within the boundaries of any given kingdom that were slaves, servants, guests, foreigners, and hired workers. Such people had some benefits of the kingdom but did not have the full rights of citizenship. Citizenship was a privilege attained by only a few of those people in the kingdom.

Roman Rule

We can learn what citizenship probably meant to the people of Jesus' day by reviewing what citizenship meant to a Roman citizen. People became citizens of the Roman Empire by birth, but citizenship was also attained by an administrative act of the Roman government. Rome, according to history, was extraordinary in its liberal grant of citizenship to people who were born in one of its territories. Historic records claim 260,000 male citizens in Rome in the year 240 B.C. At the census of Claudius in A.D. 47, the citizens were numbered at 5,984,072. Citizenship, while common, was still a fraction of the total people within the kingdom boundaries. This may well relate to Jesus' statement that many are called but few are chosen.

Initially, citizenship required all males to serve in the army. This service all but disappeared over time, resulting in an employed army run by generals but manned largely by mercenaries. Voting was reserved for a certain few who were prominent citizens. Even then, the voting of the citizenry did not wield as much power as the superior rights of the king or emperor. People who opposed the rule of the emperor could be put to death. Even citizens were subject to obedience on the penalty of death. The difference was that every citizen had certain rights to a trial before being punished. With citizenship came the security of protection from the government. Rome moved quickly to punish anyone who harmed its citizens. Pax Romana, the rule of Roman government and law, brought peace, but that peace was by the enforcement of the Roman army.

The Rule of Christ

With this background, we can contrast the kingdom of Rome as a representative of earthly kingdoms with the kingdom of heaven ruled by God. We can contrast how citizenship was obtained, what the benefits were in each kingdom, how the rule of the King was enforced, how the kingdoms spread over the earth, how promotion occurred for the citizens, and how the kingdoms were perpetuated. In doing this, I believe we will confirm the concept that the kingdom of heaven was and is primarily a spiritual realm, a

191

completely unique other-world place to live. Jesus taught about the spiritual kingdom when He met with Nicodemus as we read in John 3.

Nicodemus and Jesus Discuss the Kingdom of Heaven

In what is probably the most widely known New Testament story of all time, Jesus presented the mystery of the kingdom of heaven or kingdom of God. This is known as the story of the new birth. We find it in John 3:1-9, and it is the controlling context before John 3:16 in which Jesus explained about God's love for the world. I maintain that I had a false concept of the truth presented there for years because I read into it the tradition of my childhood, that of evangelical fundamentalism. Let me say that I have a great respect and love for my Christian upbringing, but I believe firmly now that it was immature and skewed my traditions in contrast to what the Bible really says. What if Jesus was talking about something very different from eternal life in heaven as a reward for believing certain doctrines? What might this mean to us today?

Let me quote the entire section so that we can review it now.

John 3:1-8—The New Birth

There was a man of the Pharisees named Nicodemus, a ruler of the Jews. This man came to Jesus by night and said to Him, "Rabbi, we know that You are a teacher come from God; for no one can do these signs that You do unless God is with him." Jesus answered and said to him, "Most assuredly, I say to you, unless one is born again, he cannot see the kingdom of God."

Nicodemus said to Him, "How can a man be born when he is old? Can he enter a second time into his mother's womb and be born?"

Jesus answered, "Most assuredly, I say to you, unless one is born of water and the Spirit, he cannot enter the kingdom of God. That which is born of the flesh is flesh, and that which is born of the Spirit is spirit Do not marvel that I said to you, 'You must be born again.' The wind blows where it wishes, and you hear the sound of it, but cannot tell where it comes from and where it goes. So is everyone who is born of the Spirit."

I now believe that being generated from above or from the realm of eternity is a change of sight or a change by spiritual enlightenment.

What follows are just a few comments in line with my new assumptions. Please discard for the moment what you have been taught and see if you have ears to hear what the Bible might be saying.

There is no mention of going to heaven when we die. We simply assume this to be true based on the lack of distinguishing between eternal life in heaven and the present-and-eternal kingdom of God in the here and now.

The text does not actually say "born again." The word again does not appear in the Greek text. The phrase in Greek is *gennao anothen* and is better stated, according to Strong's dictionary, "to procreate from above or from eternity." The Greek word *gennao* is often translated begat or conceived, but seldom translated born. There is another Greek word for being delivered or born. It is the misunderstanding of Nicodemus that makes us think about being born for the second time. He asked, "How can a man be born when he is old? Can he enter a second time into his mother's womb and be born?" Jesus told him this was an error. Down through the ages, humans have had a tendency for attempting to turn spiritual realities into physical things.

Please understand what I am saying here. The same Greek word translated 'born' in John 3 is translated 'conceive' in Luke's gospel where the angel told Mary about her pregnancy. Conception is a mysterious process that cannot be seen, just as is any spiritual process. Jesus was not born for some time thereafter. I maintain that our "new birth" experience is more a spiritual conception than it is a new birth or "born again" experience. One is spiritual, the other is perceived as physical, and this confused Nicodemus, too. So the 'new birth' experience and the kingdom of heaven that can be 'seen' and 'entered' are spiritual, not physical matters. The new conception from heaven and the kingdom of heaven are both primarily non-physical.

Jesus was, therefore, teaching about becoming part of a new creation, a new genus of humans who were made alive by the Spirit of God. This is what Paul described as a new creation. The Greek word, *genes,* also means "genus" or "species," and we would say today that the genes control the development of each species. We have received a graft of new genetics that will change us into something different, a child of God.

Proof that the new creation is only by the work of God comes when Jesus says, "The wind [*pneuma,* also meaning the spirit or breath of God] blows where it wishes,...so is everyone who is generated by the Spirit." (insert mine)

If the Spirit changes us by His decision, then the human decision (to accept Christ as personal Savior) is simply a conversion or change of mind. This must be preceded by regeneration by the wind of God, the Spirit of God.

How does God effect that change? By enlightenment, by causing a change of consciousness, or in Christendom we say that once we were blind, but now we see.

In this text Jesus taught that to see and to enter the present kingdom of heaven (not heaven after we die), we must have it revealed to us by spiritual enlightenment. Jesus was proclaiming the kingdom of heaven (of God), and this was what He meant by the gospel or good news. The good news is the news about the kingdom.

The question being posed in John 3 is not, are we going to heaven when we die, or, is Christ coming from heaven to rule on earth? No, the question to us is, has our consciousness, our enlightenment, our spiritual eyesight allowed us to see and enter the kingdom of God in the now, in the present? If Jesus taught us about how we see and enter the kingdom of heaven in John 3, then we can see that in Matthew 5 Jesus shared the results of living as citizens of the kingdom of heaven.

After careful study, it is my belief that the Bible does not teach that Jesus will return and establish a political kingdom for one thousand years. This theological position is not new, most reformed theologians teach this. It is called Preterism and its scholars, the Preterist, believe that most of the prophecies of the "end times" have already been fulfilled in past history. This means that the tribulation, the battle of Armageddon and the return of

194

Christ to establish His kingdom occurred in the period around 70 AD with the destruction of the temple in Jerusalem just as Jesus claimed it would. It does run contrary to the extremely popular "Left Behind" series of books that project this period into the near future.

If you expect this kingdom to be a physical one then you will be looking for His return to Israel and His reign over the earth for the Millennium. That is what I was always taught. Weren't you also taught to expect this? Let's see what John actually said in the book of Revelation. We find that what he said directly relates to what Jesus said about a spiritual reign as opposed to a physical, political reign. Where does the idea of one period of one thousand years called the Millennium come from? It comes from the English translation of the Bible.

"Blessed and holy is he who has part in the first resurrection. Over such the second death has no power, but they shall be priests of God and of Christ, and shall reign with Him a thousand years. Now when the thousand years have expired, Satan will be released from his prison" (Revelation 20:6-8). In both of these English texts the reign is said to be one thousand years. But what does the Greek word translated actually mean? What is the actual Greek word translated one thousand years?

First, the term represents a very long time that for ancient people was beyond numbering. In a similar way Peter said, "But, beloved, do not forget this one thing, that with the Lord one day is as a thousand years, and a thousand years as one day" (II Peter 3:8-9). This time frame can mean more than one thousand years. Secondly, the Greek term in Revelation is a plural word, *chilioi* (khil'-ee-oy), meaning that the word could be literally translated not just one thousand years but thousands of years. If the author had meant to limit the period to one thousand year, the word, *chili,* (single thousand) would have been used. The reign of Jesus over the spiritual kingdom of heaven is already nearly a two thousand year reign and soon will enter its third millennium. What is the practical significance of this? It means that we can see, enter, and enjoy the spiritual kingdom of heaven right now. I believe this brings new meaning to the Beatitudes of Jesus. They are not for some future day but are for right now – today. Let me explain further.

The Other-World Kingdom of Heaven and the (Beatitudes) Blessings of Citizenship

I will present the Beatitudes as descriptive statements about kingdom-of-heaven citizens. I want us to consider that they are progressive and that each description builds on the prior description. In Rome there were levels of citizenship from new citizen to a representative allowed to vote, to a member of the Senate, to the top position of Emperor. So, too, there are levels of kingdom-of-heaven citizenship. Each beatitude presents a different spiritual level.

The Blessings of the Kingdom of Heaven Are Levels of Spiritual Maturity

The movement from entry to top rank in the kingdom of heaven is what we also know as spiritual formation. We confuse spiritual discipline with spiritual formation. Spiritual formation comes from within and is fully the work of the Spirit. It is done to us and in us and not by us. The opposite is spiritual development wherein we work out certain spiritual disciplines like prayer and Bible study, fasting and self-denial. These have a show of spirituality but may only be works of our flesh if they are not based on the internal spiritual formation of God within us.

I believe the descriptive statements in the Beatitudes as found in the book of Matthew are also stages of spiritual maturity, levels of enlightenment, and changes of understanding or consciousness. They involve ever-increasing enlightenment. They will be presented here as stages of spirituality:

- Stage One—"Blessed are the poor in spirit, for theirs is the kingdom of heaven."
- Stage Two—"Blessed are those who mourn, for they shall be comforted."
- Stage Three—"Blessed are the meek, for they shall inherit the earth."

196

- Stage Four—"Blessed are those who hunger and thirst after righteousness, for they shall be filled."
- Stage Five—"Blessed are the merciful, for they shall obtain mercy."
- Stage Six—"Blessed are the pure in heart, for they shall see God."
- Stage Seven—"Blessed are the peacemakers, for they shall be called sons of God."
- Stage Eight—"Blessed are those who are persecuted for righteousness sake, for theirs is the kingdom of heaven."
- Stage Nine—"Blessed are you when they revile and persecute you and say all kinds of evil against you falsely for My sake. Rejoice and be exceedingly glad, for great is your reward in heaven, for so they persecuted the prophets before you."

The Kingdom of Heaven Is Absolutely Antithetical to the Realm of the Natural World

I want to point out that every beatitude presents an unnatural way for humans to think and live. Each one is paradoxical. Each one presents a challenge that will require supernatural power for that level of spiritually empowered living in this world. Each one, therefore, requires the fulfillment by the Spirit of Christ within us. We cannot achieve this level of living. Only Jesus, our older brother, ever lived at this level of spirituality. We are, however, able to live abundantly, above and beyond what we could ever think or ask, if we recognize the incarnate Son lives within us to provide the desire and the power for this unique form of consciousness and level of living. This is why each level promises us blessing—to be supremely fortunate, well off, happy, blessed, or beatified. I believe that putting on this kingdom citizenship way of living is putting on the mind of Christ.

In 1 Corinthians 2:14-16 Paul said it this way, "For the natural man does not receive the things of the Spirit of God, for they are foolishness to him; nor can he know them, because they are spiritually discerned. But he who is spiritual judges all things, yet he himself is rightly judged by no man. For who has known the

197

mind of the Lord, that he may instruct Him. But we have the mind of Christ."

To have the mind of Christ is to think like Jesus, and to think like Him is to live like Him. We are privileged to have the very thoughts of Jesus on how to enter and how to progress in kingdom-of-heaven living. I hope that the following sketches of insights into the mind of Christ and illustrations will challenge all of us to attainment of advanced citizenship roles in the kingdom of heaven (God).

Let's look at the stages of spiritual development as Jesus presented them in the Beatitudes. In this review we will discover why citizens of the kingdom of heaven are developing in stage after stage of bliss or blessedness. The kingdom of heaven is a transcendent spiritual kingdom, and because it is an other-world realm, its citizens value and are motivated by unseen spiritual forces that cause them to change from natural human beings into supernatural human beings—becoming like Christ and sharing in the resources of the sons of God.

Stage One—Blessed are the poor in spirit, for theirs is the kingdom of heaven.

This first stage is our citizenship entrance requirement into the kingdom of heaven. We must again become as children, poor in spirit. Little children have not yet developed independent egos. They cannot separate their identities from others'. Mother is an extension of the baby, just as the baby was once a part of the mother in the embryonic stage. Likewise, our adult concept of separation and independence from God must be shattered to return us to oneness. Jesus said it this way in Mark 10:15: "Assuredly I say to you, whoever does not receive the kingdom of God as a little child will by no means enter it." We find that not only must the independent ego be shattered, but the consciousness that is the result of sin, separation from God, must be replaced with the absolute assurance of unity with God. It is the equivalent of the return to Eden, the return to the mother's womb.

Stage Two—Blessed are those who mourn, for they shall be comforted.

In this second stage we must learn to overcome false expectations in this life and accept earthly life as it is. In our human childhood we tended to believe that life would be great for us. We believed in a magical Santa Claus who would give us whatever we wanted if we were good little boys and girls. Life, however, soon taught us that our good behavior does not always directly relate to our blessings. We slowly discovered that God's promise is not always for His blessings but sometimes simply for His presence, strength, and comfort when we mourn. Jesus taught it this way in John 16:33:"In this world you will have tribulation; but be of good cheer [fear not], I have overcome the world." In the midst of trials, testing, and suffering, we find that the comfort of God, the knowledge of His unfailing love, carries us to a higher kingdom level. His love perfected in us casts out any fear. We discover that love is learning to let go of fear.

Stage Three—Blessed are the meek, for they shall inherit the earth.

We try so hard to control our lives by our own power, but then we learn the lesson that the last shall be first, that the leader must be servant of all. We discover that we cannot take the role of ruler or leader in the kingdom for ourselves; it is only given to the poor in spirit—the meek person. Matthew 5:5 tells us, "Blessed are the meek for they shall inherit the earth." Jesus ruled His spiritual kingdom in humility, and His humble Spirit now must rule over us. We remember that He was not from a famous family. He had no endorsement from His religious leaders. He never graduated from a school or seminary. He did not start a church, denomination, or movement. And He never traveled outside the small nation, about one hundred miles long. He accomplished earning the right to be King of kings by simply showing the love of God and doing good wherever He went. Wouldn't this be a light and easy burden for us as leaders in His kingdom? This will lead to bliss, the simplicity of spirituality—all is love.

Stage Four—Blessed are those who hunger and thirst after righteousness, for they shall be filled.

We reach this stage when we begin to learn about incarnational spirituality—Christ in you the hope of glory. We

199

have His righteousness accredited to us and then produced in us. We thirst no more because as Jesus promised the woman at the well, we have a spring of living water coming from our spirit. It is very interesting that Jesus launched his public ministry at a wedding party by being very gracious to the wedding host and the bride and groom. He gave the gift of new wine, enhancing the joy of celebration. In Matthew 11:19 we read, "The Son of Man came eating and drinking, and they say, 'Look, a gluttonous man and a winebibber.'" Jesus, we see, was into parties—His joy was overflowing.

We should take note of the reason for the water pots at the wedding feast. These six large water pots were for ceremonial cleaning—washing the guests and the dishes. Six is symbolic as the number that represents mankind. The ceremonial, cleansing waters spoke of the need to remove the stains of sin. Jesus, however, replaced the washing away of sins with the wine of celebration! New wine speaks of the new, indwelling Spirit of Christ that produces His life within us. The master of the wedding feast, after tasting the wine, proclaims, "You have saved the best for last!" Jesus came to replace the sin consciousness that leads to believing we are separated from God with a life consciousness. We are one with Him, and we contain the Living Water that becomes new wine. This is a blessing so good that most Christians cannot receive it.

Hebrews 10:2 says, "For the worshipers once purified, would have had no more consciousness of sins." Are you reveling in your personal new wine, or are you still using the old wash water?

Stage Five—Blessed are the merciful, for they shall obtain mercy.

Giving mercy demands forgiveness; obtaining mercy means we accept forgiveness. Living in mercy and granting forgiveness means we fully accept and consistently grant forgiveness to everyone by agreeing with Jesus—"They know not what they do." Once we are enlightened to the forgiving heart of Jesus, we no longer can hold a grudge or try to get even. We know that Jesus said in His Lord's Prayer, "Forgive us our debts as we forgive our debtors." We not only want our sins and errors forgiven, we want to let that forgiveness and mercy we have received flow out to others so that they, too, will enjoy the blessings of living in mercy. We begin to know we have reached this state of blessing when the time between the infraction of our rights and the time when we extend forgiveness shortens to only moments. No one holding a grudge is happy. Merciful persons are happy-kingdom citizens.

Stage Six—Blessed are the pure in heart, for they shall see God.

The heart motive is changed in life to look for God or good in everything. The pure in heart have purity exhibited in their motives even when actions falter. Life becomes an exciting God hunt to discover His presence even in the midst of suffering. Every person who "saw" God, Isaiah, Job, John, Moses, all understood that they were unfit to stand in His presence. We, however, have been made fit in our relationship with Christ Jesus; we have His perfect righteousness given us as a gift. Our hearts become pure when we drop our judgmental attitude that has always trapped us into judging everything as black or white, good or evil. Our hearts become pure, and we see God in everything. Then we can see that even human evil perpetrated against us is coming from an immature heart in another person—a life based on fear, not on love. We remember that we, too, were once just like that. Like our Master, Jesus, we can come to say as Jesus did in John 19:11 at the trial leading to His crucifixion, "You could have no power at all against Me unless it had been given you from above. Therefore, the one who delivered Me to you has the greater sin." And I believe that God the Father could see from heaven and smiled, because Jesus displayed in His life of faith the knowledge that God is in everything—good or evil.

Stage Seven—Blessed are the peacemakers, for they shall be called sons of God.

The unreasonable peace (that comes from knowing that God is in control of everything) in the lives of these advanced citizens overflows onto others, bringing peace even to one's enemies. These warriors of light now wage peace rather than war. The power of peace sets apart the two kinds of warriors: warriors of peacekeeping and warriors of peacemaking. To make peace

201

requires that we set aside our judgmental attitude and learn not to speak as much as we listen. Jesus set the standard for this seventh stage by His teaching in Matthew 7:1-2: "Judge not, that you be not judged. For with what judgment you judge, you will be judged; and with the same measure you use, it will be measured back to you." To live non-judgmentally, one must give up the knee-jerk comparisons that cause us to react critically. Peace from Jesus comes with the non-judging and affirming attitude that wants more to understand than to be understood. Does this lack of judging characterize your life and mine?

Stage Eight—Blessed are those who are persecuted for righteousness sake, for theirs is the kingdom of heaven.

The incarnation of Christ is now so complete in these kingdom citizens that tribulations and persecutions are not only expected but seen as opportunities to be Christ among their enemies. I know I still tend to hate my enemies and that loving them is a major stretch for me. Obviously, I need the incarnation of the Spirit of Christ to love like He loved. If you doubt the demand of Jesus, remember His word in Matthew 5:44-45, "I say to you, love your enemies, bless those who curse you, do good to those who hate you, and pray for those who spitefully use you and persecute you that you may be sons of your Father in heaven; for He makes His sun rise on the evil and the good, and sends rain on the just and the unjust."

Unbelievable! Obviously, the way we take sides and put down and kill our enemies is diametrically opposed to the kingdom-of-heaven teaching. Again, this level of spirituality will demand reliance on His love within us.

Your joyful Master, Jesus, is eager to have you fully enter His spiritual kingdom that is being formed within you right now, one in which you will live at peace and with joy, above the conflicts of this world. Are you ready to celebrate kingdom life with the blessed, blissful, joyful Jesus?

I have spent over fifteen years counseling hundreds of Christian laypeople, pastors, and missionaries. I have had the privilege of sharing the claims of Christ with many who did not profess Him as their Savior and Lord. I have to say that the people of the world are less troubled on average than the people of the church. I believe that Christian people long for the promises of Jesus to be real in their lives but find, instead, that they are constantly reminded of how far they fall short. This leads to guilt and frustration unknown in the world.

Further, the church has specialized in making good church members who are religious enough to perpetuate the church. We have, however, as my subtitle suggests, buried the gospel under tons of religious rubble. We are trained enough to teach, usher, sing, and tithe, but we are almost nothing like Jesus in our attitudes and lifestyles.

Unfortunately, church leadership cannot lead members to a level of spirituality if they, themselves, have never experienced or attained it. I am convinced that if Jesus returned today, He would find many churches dominated by legalistic leaders, men and women of whom the Pharisees would have been proud to call their own! Jesus would find great numbers of people who attend church but whose spiritual lives are lukewarm, the kind that make Him want to spit them out of His mouth (Rev. 3). Who knows, Jesus might agree with the critics who discount our churches and say we are "mostly just a bunch of hypocrites." We must listen to the words of Jesus who said in Matthew 21:31, "Assuredly I say to you that tax collectors [cheating traitors] and harlots [prostitutes] enter the kingdom of God before you."

Wouldn't it be a shame if Jesus returned to Denver today and had to say, "Assuredly I say to you that many of these New Agers, Gays and Hookers are entering the kingdom before you religious people?" Can you now believe this?

Stage Nine—Stages eight and nine are very similar. I do not want to attempt a full definition of the difference here. Briefly, these saints see themselves in unity with all the past prophets. This stage transcends time and connects this stage of spirituality to eternity.

Please Interact with the Author

If you have been challenged and blessed by this book, I hope that you will look forward with me to the next one. Christ has laid upon my heart the further presentation of the description of the kingdom of heaven within us, the practices of religious Christianity that have blocked the entrance for millions of frustrated believers, and the way that God is spreading His kingdom in and also around the church. His will cannot be frustrated. Listen to this final challenge from Hebrews 12:28: "Therefore, since we are receiving a kingdom which cannot be shaken, let us have grace, by which we may serve God acceptably with reverence and godly fear."

Dear brothers and sisters, this kingdom of heaven is invincible; it cannot be shaken. What a place of refuge and citizenship! I believe God's Spirit has prompted me to write the next book entitled *Butterfly Believers*, a transformational approach to Spiritual Formation. In *Butterfly Believers* I hope to present a different way of interpreting and understanding the New Testament concepts of the kingdom of heaven and the Beatitudes in the hope that we will be better able to see and immediately enter the kingdom of heaven as a living reality.

I trust that you already have a thirst for more of this kingdom teaching. If so, email me at twmesser@comcast.net. I would be pleased to answer your questions or to suggest other materials that you might want to read. Please visit our web sites:

http://conceptpublishing.org

At this site you will find details about this book and the objectives of the publisher, Concept Publishing, Inc. There are articles you can read and download on other similar topics about grace and freedom. New books will be featured on this site as they become available. Each book or article will be encouraging, informative, and will present new or improved paradigms about our freedom in the grace of Christ.

http://higherfreedom.com

This site features application of our freedom in Christ. We explore freedom emotionally, spiritually, relationally and even financially, and give resources designed to release you to become all that you can be.

Interactive Discussion Questions

1. Has the Kingdom of Heaven been a mystery to you so far?
2. Why do you suppose Jesus was always talking about what we rarely talk about?
3. Is your life happy or blissful? Do you think in terms of being a blessed believer?
4. How might it change you if your heart were to be set on the spiritual kingdom of heaven and not so much on the religious practices of the church?
5. Why do humans want to place emphasis on the physical realm? (For example, the emphasis on the church in our day and the political reign of Rome over Israel and the beautiful temple in Jerusalem in Bible times.)
6. Why do we want to emphasize human free will over the sovereignty of God?
7. What is the connection between the kingdom and the sovereignty of the king?
8. If we have the mind of Christ and rely upon it, how will this impact our living?
9. How do you react to Jesus saying that tax-collectors and harlots enter the kingdom before you, and the author's application to new-age people, prostitutes, and homosexuals entering the kingdom before us?
10. Does the teaching of the kingdom of heaven cause you pride or humility?
11. Do you hold onto your old ways out of love or out of fear?

Notes:

Individual Stages of Human Development and Perception and Their Correlation to History:

Stages	Belief	**Historic Biblical Era**
1—Womb	Mom and I are one	Garden of Eden
2—Baby	Mom is my source	Babylon—worship of the woman goddess
3—Child	Father (Santa) is source	Abraham—worship of a male God
4—Teen	I become my own source	Moses—Era of Law - control new freedom
5—Worker/ Warrior	My leader is my source	Judges and kings— Human leaders as source
6—Citizen	My nation is my source	David—Israel is my source (physical king)
7—Wounded Healer	God is my source	Jesus—Christ is my source (psychological king)
8—Wise Old Sage	God and I are one	Universal Body – His spiritual body, is my source

Notes:

The mystery of our human union with God and sense of separation from Him causes some potential theological debate and concerns. I want to contrast three levels – the physical, the psychological, and the spiritual.

First, in the physical created sense, everything that is contains His spirit, or we might say from the view of science that God's Spirit and energy is the same thing. All energy in the physical universe is from the pre-creation God. Before the creation, or what science calls the big bang, I believe there was God, and God is pure energy. Both God and energy are eternal in that God and energy cannot be created or destroyed. I believe that every vision of God presents Him as brilliant light, just like energy.

All material things, all matter, is simply energy held in a complex formation. When matter is 'destroyed' it returns to its original energy. In this sense, what Paul said when he quoted the Greek poet was that "in Him we live and move and have our being." This physical level of creation displays the obvious; when God is not holding it together, all the matter in the universe will return to energy. Our physical being is therefore dependent upon God for its existence. At the highest level of consciousness, the wise old sage stage, the physical person becomes much less important and the spiritual, eternal person becomes the focus. This, I believe, is what John meant when he described the elder in this way, "I write to you, fathers, because you have known Him who is from the beginning." I believe John was saying that the fathers know the Eternal One. Here the word 'known" means 'are intimately connected to Him', just as we know each other intimately in marriage and are thus said to be one.

The second level of union I will call the union of grace. This level relates more directly to the soul, the psychological or personality of man. Original creation was an act of grace in the sense that it was a gift. Material things and creatures did not create themselves. They were given their being from God. We, however, think of grace as the gift of salvation and the gift of empowerment to live the Christ-like life. When we received the gift of the Holy

Spirit it did not directly affect our physical being. The change of our body awaits our death/resurrection transfer from time and space into what we call heaven. Heaven is the eternal realm, the home of the pre-creation and 'pre-big bang' God. I believe it is less a place and more a new dimension outside of time/space/matter, because a place denotes created space.

Scripture teaches us that Adam was made of the dust of the Earth. This related to the formation of his physical body from earth or matter. God then breathed into Adam the breath of life. The breath of God is understood in the Old Testament as the spirit of God. God energized the dust. What did it become? Adam received the breath of life and became a living soul. The soul of man is also what was impacted by The Fall, or Adam's choice. He chose independent life and became personally aware of a sense of fear and separation from God. Certainly God did not withdraw His spirit by removing living energy from Adam or he would have physically died that day. The penalty God gave in advance was, "in the day you eat it (the fruit of that tree) you shall surely die." Something died that day, but it was not physical death, the return of the spirit or 'breath' of God, because Adam lived for many years thereafter.

Scripture claims that the soul that sins shall die. Obviously, the commission of a sin does not directly and physically kill us at the time of the act. How then could God say that Adam died that day?

Now we turn to the third level. It was a death in the sense that the Spirit breathed into Adam no longer was directly connected to his soul life (his mind, will, and emotions). Paul later taught that pre-regeneration we were all dead in our trespasses and sins. This does not mean that God has taken His Spirit from us, but that we have disconnected His indwelling Spirit and our spirit from control of our souls. We then 'live' in a state of spiritual 'death.' Death does not mean we do not exist; it means we exist without connectedness to God, the source of life.

The gift of grace God gave to us in Christ reconnects the life, or spirit, or energy of God in us. Our souls no longer need to live in a state of fear and sense of disconnection from God. The gift of grace reconnects us in regard to our souls, but it also empowers us to live in the original design of a human being in the image of God. Grace gives us salvation, the restored image of God, as well as empowerment. The Apostle Paul stated the problem clearly, and the problem is and was within us. We sinned and felt separated from God, but His Spirit as energizing life never left us. Think carefully about what Paul said in Col. 1:21-22, "And you, who once were alienated and <u>enemies in your mind</u> (emphasis mine) by wicked works, yet now He has reconciled in the body of His flesh through death, to present you holy, and blameless, and above reproach in His sight." I believe this is the major point of the gospel. We need conversion, a change of mind. Adam and Eve had the same problem. They hid from God when He, in fact, went looking for them. The separation was primarily in their minds, not in the mind of God.

The message of Jesus in the gospel takes away the focus on the wrath of God and replaces it with the image of the loving Father. God did not really change. What changed was mans understanding of God. As Paul taught, God was in Christ reconciling the world unto Himself NOT COUNTING THEIR SINS AGAINST THEM. If we believe this we are reconnected in our souls and have a changed or renewed mind, no longer thinking we are enemies but knowing that we are beloved children of God. I ask, Are we there yet? Do we have this kind of understanding and consciousness? To know and be one with God is the highest level of consciousness. It restores and even improves the original human condition of Adam in Eden.

Oneness, or union with God, does not make us equal to God. He is vastly greater than we are. You might say that my big toe is one with my body, but alone my toe is dramatically simpler and less than the entire me. Ultimate human oneness with God awaits our eventual union with Him in the eternal spiritual realm. Paul calls this eternal hope "the riches of the glory of His inheritance in the saints." Evidently Christ looks forward to receiving His gift from His Father – the saints united with Christ in God.

I see three levels of union and three stages of our salvation: salvation of the body which is future and awaits the replacement of the physical body with a spiritual body; the salvation of the soul which is current, ongoing, and a process by which our minds are renewed, our wills submitted and our emotions brought to peace, and finally salvation of the spirit when we are made spiritually alive at regeneration. The soul is continually being saved by an ongoing process called progressive sanctification. The spirit was 'dead' in the sense that it was turned off when man went his own way and became independent and separate in his thinking.

Picture it as something like a lamp that is plugged in to electricity by a cord but has no light because the switch is off. Our transformation into the image of God and the nature of Christ is dependent on a renewed mind according to Paul. We believe ourselves separated from God because we are guilty of sins, fear His punishment, and hide in shame. All of this is our reaction to God, who loves us so much that He comes looking for us. Separation, or lack of union, is our thinking problem now that Christ has reconciled us to God who is NOT COUNTING OUR SINS AGAINST US.

According to Peter in 2 Peter 1:3-4, "His divine power has given to us all things that pertain to life and godliness, through the knowledge of Him who called us by glory and virtue, by which have been given to us exceedingly great and precious promises, that through these you may be partakers of the Divine Nature, having escaped the corruption that is in the world through lust." (emphasis mine). I can say I partake of the Divine Nature without saying I am God. I believe this is what the restored image of God means.

Returning to Mars Hill with Paul we find that he taught in Acts 17:28-30, "as also some of your own poets have said, 'For we are also His offspring.' Therefore, since we are the offspring of God, we ought not to think that the Divine Nature is like gold or silver or stone, something shaped by art and man's devising." It is the wise old sage who has the wisdom to know that the spiritual realm (being the offspring of God) is the eternal and therefore ultimate reality. Gold, silver, and art in the physical realm might represent the spiritual realm, but they do not contain the ultimate Divine Nature which Paul agreed comes to mankind by our being His (God's) offspring, His children.

In summary: We are one with God in that:

1) His Spirit, or Energy, sustains us and all creation. This means we have physical unity.
2) We are slowly becoming conformed to the image of Christ as our souls, or personalities, reflect Him. This is increasing psychological unity, also known as the unity of grace.
3) Spiritually we are new creatures in Christ. Paul said, "Christ in you is the hope of glory." This is spiritual unity.
4) This three leveled unity does not make us God because it depends entirely upon Him for its source. Without Him we are simply human, existing only at a near intelligent animal level. With Him we are new creations in Christ and the restored Adamic beings made in the image and likeness of God.

2804086

Made in the USA